ARIES
21 MARCH – 20 APRIL

First published in Great Britain 2011
by Mills & Boon, an imprint of Harlequin (UK) Limited,
Eton House, 18-24 Paradise Road, Richmond, Surrey TW9 1SR

Copyright © Dadhichi Toth 2011

ISBN: 978 0 263 89651 0

Design by Jo Yuen Graphic Design
Typeset by KDW DESIGNS

Harlequin (UK) policy is to use papers that are natural, renewable and recyclable products and made from wood grown in sustainable forests. The logging and manufacturing processes conform to the legal environmental regulations of the country of origin.

Printed and bound in Spain
by Blackprint CPI, Barcelona

Dedicated to

The Light of Intuition

Sri V. Krishnaswamy—mentor and friend

With thanks to

Joram and Isaac

Special thanks to

Nyle Cruz for

initial creative layouts and ongoing support

⊁ ABOUT DADHICHI ⊁

Dadhichi is one of Australia's foremost astrologers and is frequently seen on television and in other media. He has the unique ability to draw from complex astrological theory to provide clear, easily understandable advice and insights for people who want to know what their futures may hold.

In the 26 years that Dadhichi has been practising astrology, face reading and other esoteric studies, he has conducted over 10,000 consultations. His clients include celebrities, political and diplomatic figures, and media and corporate identities from all over the world.

Dadhichi's unique blend of astrology and face reading helps people fulfil their true potential. His extensive experience practising Western astrology is complemented by his research into the theory and practice of Eastern forms of astrology.

Dadhichi has been a guest on many Australian television shows, and several of his political and worldwide forecasts have proved uncannily accurate. He appears regularly on Australian television networks and is a columnist for online and offline Australian publications.

His websites—www.dadhichi.com and www.facereader.com—attract hundreds of thousands of visitors each month, and offer a wide variety of features, helpful information and services.

MESSAGE FROM DADHICHI

Hello once again and welcome to your 2012 horoscope book!

Can you believe it's already 2012? Time flies by so quickly and now here we are in this fateful year, a time for which several religions of the world—including the Mayans from 3100BC—have predicted some extraordinary events that are supposedly going to affect us all!

Some people are worried there will be a physical cataclysm that will kill millions and millions. Some are of the opinion it is the end of the economic and social models we have lived by for thousands of years. Others seem to believe the Planet Nibiru will whiz by planet Earth and beam up the 144,000 Chosen Ones.

Whatever the opinion, it is an undeniable fact that we are experiencing some remarkable worldwide changes due to global warming (even though that remains a point of contention) and other societal shifts. Scientific knowledge continues to outrun our ability to keep up with it, and time appears to be moving faster and faster.

But my own research has categorically led me to repeat: 'Relax, everyone; it is *not* the end of the world!' There will most certainly be a backlash at some point by Mother Earth at the gross unconsciousness of many of us. There will be ravaging storms, earthquakes and other meteorological phenomena that will shake the Earth, hopefully waking up those of us still in a deep sleep, dreaming, or possibly even sleepwalking. It is time to open our eyes and take responsibility.

If there are any significant global changes I foresee, they are the emergence of wider self-government and the greater Aquarian qualities of the coming New Age. This period is the cusp or changeover between the Age of Pisces, the Fish, and the Age of Aquarius, the Dawn of Higher Mankind.

Astrology, and these small books I write about it, are for the sole purpose of shedding light on our higher selves, alerting us to the need to evolve, step up to the plate, and assume responsibility for our thoughts, words and deeds, individually and collectively. The processes of karma are ripe now as we see the Earth's changes shouting to us about our past mistakes as a civilisation.

I hope you gain some deeper insight into yourself through these writings. For the 2012 series I have extended the topics and focused more on relationships. It is only through having a clear perception of our responsibility towards others that we can live the principles of astrology and karma to reach our own self-actualisation, both as individuals and as a race.

I hope you see the light of truth within yourself and that these words will act as a pointer in your ongoing search.

All the best for 2012.

Your Astrologer,

www.dadhichi.com
dadhichitoth@gmail.com
Tel: +61 (0) 413 124 809

❧ CONTENTS ❧

Aries Profile

Aries Snapshot   12

Aries Overview   15

Aries Cusps   18

Aries Celebrities   22

Aries at Large

Aries Man   28

Aries Woman   32

Aries Child   35

Aries Lover   38

Aries Friend   41

Aries Enemy   43

Aries at Home

Home Front   46

Karma, Luck and Meditation   49

Health, Wellbeing and Diet   51

Finance Finesse   53

⊁ CONTENTS ⊁

Aries at Work

Aries Career   56

Aries Boss   58

Aries Employee   60

Professional Relationships: Best and Worst   63

Aries in Love

Romantic Compatibility   68

Horoscope Compatibility for Aries   72

Aries Partnerships   76

Platonic Relationships: Best and Worst   80

Sexual Relationships: Best and Worst   84

Quiz: Have You Found Your Perfect Match?   89

2012: Yearly Overview

Key Experiences   96

Romance and Friendship   97

Work and Money   101

Health, Beauty and Lifestyle   108

Karma, Spirituality and Emotional Balance   113

CONTENTS
CONTINUED

2012: Monthly and Daily Predictions

January	116
February	122
March	128
April	134
May	140
June	145
July	150
August	155
September	160
October	167
November	174
December	181

2012: Astronumerology

The Power Behind Your Name	190
Your Planetary Ruler	197
Your Planetary Forecast	199

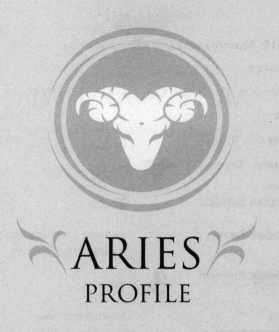

ARIES

PROFILE

THERE IS ONLY ONE SUCCESS—TO
SPEND YOUR LIFE IN YOUR OWN
WAY.

Christopher Morley

✂ ARIES SNAPSHOT ✂

Key Life Phrase		I Am
Zodiac Totem		The Ram
Zodiac Symbol		♈
Zodiac Facts		First sign of the zodiac; moveable, hot and dry
Zodiac Element		Fire
Key Characteristics		Determined, fiery, executive skills, born leader, impulsive, headstrong, opinionated, loyal, physical, driven, ambitious
Compatible Star Signs		Leo, Taurus, Sagittarius and Gemini
Mismatched Signs		Cancer, Virgo, Libra and Capricorn

Ruling Planet		Mars
Love Planets	❤	Sun and Venus
Finance Planet	💵	Venus
Speculation Planet		Sun
Career Planets	👤	Saturn and Mercury
Spiritual and Karmic Planets	🪷	Jupiter and the Sun
Friendship Planet		Uranus
Destiny Planet		Sun
Famous Arians	★★	Elle Macpherson, Ashley Judd, Kate Hudson, Vincent van Gogh, Michael York, Mariah Carey, Elton John, James Caan, Diana Ross, Russell Crowe, William Hurt, Marlon Brando, Aretha Franklin, Sarah Jessica Parker, Francis Ford Coppola, David Frost, Omar Sharif, David Letterman, Steven Seagal, Charlie Chaplin, Celine Dion and Hugh Hefner

Lucky Numbers and Significant Years	1, 3, 9, 10, 12, 18, 19, 27, 28, 30, 36, 37, 45, 46, 48, 54, 55, 57, 63, 64, 65, 72, 73, 75, 82 and 83
Lucky Gems	Red coral, carnelian, pearl, yellow sapphire, golden topaz and garnet
Lucky Fragrances	Rose, ylang ylang, jasmine, rosemary, pine and clary sage
Affirmation/ Mantra	I am the best, yet I am humble
Lucky Days	Monday, Tuesday, Thursday and Sunday

⚹ ARIES OVERVIEW ⚹

Speed, power and a distinctive presence are the hallmarks of a typical Aries. Someone born under your star sign doesn't slip by without being noticed and sometimes this can be a little intimidating for others. Not everyone has quite as much influence or control as you do, remember that.

You're a born leader and people are quite aware of this. However, when others first meet you, your presence can take them by surprise. Often your desire to share, take the lead, and instigate new and exciting ideas is misinterpreted as arrogance. If this message is conveyed to you, you're surprised because you don't necessarily want to dominate others. Not consciously, anyway.

Aries is a fire sign: life to you is a journey of excitement, adventure and discovery. You like to get out there–to test life and your own ability by taking things to the limits of your endurance. This is where others sometimes don't keep up with you. You believe in the theory of survival of the fittest, and those who can keep up with you gain your respect. Unfortunately, those who don't keep up usually fall by the wayside.

Although you don't always consciously try to dominate, you are competitive in the way you live your life and need ways to express this actively, without treading on other people's toes. You certainly enjoy winning and you do all you can to come out on top. For this reason you are seen as a successful person and someone to look up to. You are admired by those with whom you work and play.

SECRET ARIES...

*Aries display great strength and power on the outside,
but are soft on the inside. Aries dread a submissive role
anywhere, anytime. It just isn't in your nature. But
you are actually quite loving!*

You find it hard dealing with situations where there's no spark of energy or excitement, and it's probably this factor that makes you as competitive and driven as you are. A goal wouldn't seem quite as alluring to you if it were otherwise. It's the thrill of the journey that attracts you, Aries.

Honesty is another thing that people should get used to when dealing with you. You pride yourself on integrity and, even if you come across as brutal in your candid opinions, you'd rather be disliked than regarded as a dishonest character. With you, Aries, what people see is what they get.

Ambition is built into your personality, and this applies as much to your personal affairs as it does your business and professional life. You are uncompromising, determined and focused on what you wish to achieve. In fact, when the going gets tough, you tend to crank things up a notch and enjoy the challenge just to prove you can overcome any and all obstacles.

Fearless Aries

You are fearless and inspire others. It's hard to tell whether your courage is bravery or impulsive hot-headedness. You are a leader and, if you were in a shipwreck or survival situation, you'd be the first to throw your hat in the ring for the role to lead other survivors to safety.

Try to exercise more patience when it comes to dealing with your friends and loved ones. In your desire and enthusiasm to finish what you begin, you often find things are moving too slowly. You are frequently reckless in trying to reach the finishing line.

In respect of this, don't push others beyond their limits. Tempering your expectations will be one of the main lessons you'll need to learn in life. Your co-workers, family members and, in particular, your children may not be able to keep up with your hectic lifestyle and often-demanding level of exertion. Just because you can do something doesn't mean everyone around you is as capable. You should try harder to help people compassionately without being too severe on them.

ARIES CUSPS

ARE YOU A CUSP BABY?

Being born on the changeover of two star signs means you have the qualities of both. Sometimes you don't know whether you're Arthur or Martha, as they say! Some of my clients can't quite figure out if they are indeed their own star sign, or the one before, or after. This is to be expected because being born on the borderline means you take on aspects of both. The following outlines give an overview of the subtle effects of these cusp dates and how they affect your personality quite significantly.

Aries–Pisces Cusp

The intensity, fire and drive of your typical Aries Sun sign is significantly softened by the Piscean influence. This means that if you're born in the first week or so of Aries—between the 21st and the 28th of March—you are called a cusp baby, and will be influenced not only by Mars and Aries, but also by Jupiter, Neptune and the sign that they rule, namely Pisces.

There is a danger that you are too impulsive in giving your assistance to others and you will often kick yourself when that advantage is taken too far. You realise afterwards that you are an easy target and people do indeed take you for a ride. This will, of course, make you very angry once you realise what a fool you have been. Try to assess the character and motives of others more carefully before quickly giving over your time, money or heart.

Although you still have the drive and determination of your Aries Sun sign, you're also influenced by compassionate and loving Pisces. Your heart reaches out to others and you feel the suffering and pain of your fellow human beings. You're able to empathise and are therefore a great listener when it comes to others wanting to share their problems with you. You never turn others away and this is why you're loved by all your friends and family.

It may be difficult choosing between your head and your heart at times. Making decisions may not always be easy when you eventually realise that jumping the gun has caused you to make errors of judgement. But although you need to hold back at times, you also run the risk of becoming a procrastinator by swinging too far in the opposite direction.

Try to balance your emotional and mental assessments of people and your life's direction. Eventually you'll find the perfect balance between your head and heart.

An important life lesson for you will be to trust in the process of life and not get too caught up in the decision-making process itself. Get your facts, get some feedback from those you trust—even those who are perhaps professionals—and then make a decision. Once this is done, however, you must let go and let life determine the outcome.

Aries–Taurus Cusp

The independent nature that is so predominantly a feature of your Aries character is heightened by being born at the tail end of your Sun sign. The next sign of the zodiac is Taurus and if you were born between the 13th and the 20th of April you will exhibit many of the traits of the Bull.

Dependable, sometimes stubborn, but always loving, your combined Sun sign of Aries and Taurus makes you are very reliable character indeed. You have a tenacity coupled with creative enterprise that can make you a very successful person; not just in your professional endeavours, but your personal affairs as well. You're always loyal to a 'T', and this you take from both Sun signs.

Taurus-born individuals are very security conscious, so you will always make an effort to ensure your future financial circumstances are comfortable and leave very little to chance. Because you have such a high level of Aries energy, your industriousness along with your tenacity and dependability make you an awesome force to be dealt with.

You will always have money and, even if in the early stages of your life you are not super wealthy, you will slowly but surely grow your nest egg, which will hold you in good stead later in life.

One life lesson that you must heed is that of flexibility. You will run into many difficulties if you hold on to your position too strongly in the face of good advice. You must learn when to let go, when change is necessary and, most importantly, when you are wrong. By letting your ego get the better of you, you will suffer setbacks in your personal relationships. Humility is one of the important key words for those of you born in this Aries and Taurus cuspal time of the year.

✖ ARIES CELEBRITIES ✖

FAMOUS MALE:
QUENTIN TARANTINO

Wow, what a trailblazer as far as moviemaking is concerned! Quentin reflects the originality and sometimes prankish Aries nature through his moviemaking.

Interestingly, many of his films feature violence and blood-drenched scenes. The colour red, which is notoriously Aries in nature, also seems to depict his astrological sign very well.

The fact that Quentin Tarantino has created a genre of film that is unique to him attests to the fact that Aries is original and progressive in many respects. Perhaps the violent aspects of these movies are his way of expressing the pent-up anger, irritability and sometimes violent facets of the Arian nature. At least he is finding a suitable outlet that is acceptable and which has also won him worldwide acclaim.

If you were to speak to Quentin Tarantino, he would most certainly exhibit the independent and liberal qualities of the first sign of the zodiac—

Aries. You can see this through his films, which are blatantly honest and, in most ways, no respecter of persons.

> *Although Tarantino seems to focus a great deal on the darker aspects of human nature, he is able to do it cleverly with humour. Aries-born like him usually have an uncanny knack of being able to mix serious ideas with humorous and quirky methods. That's probably because Aries have the planet Mercury ruling their minds, and this planet is notorious for impish and comical behaviour.*

In his masterpiece *Inglourious Basterds*, Quentin exhibits the extremes of his artistic brilliance by coupling ruthless violence with subtle comic relief, which makes this movie an extraordinarily fascinating one. This is reflective of his most extraordinary Aries personality.

Quentin will go on to do other great films, and will surely continue to make even greater strides in progressing the film industry through his unique contributions. Aries like Quentin are always leaders and never followers.

FAMOUS FEMALE:
VICTORIA BECKHAM

Victoria leads an active, famous and sometimes hectic lifestyle which, like Quentin Tarantino, is also a unique Aries star sign trait. Being born under the first sign of the zodiac means she is restless and never likes to stay in one spot. As such, is it any wonder she made her name as a dancer and a singer with the pop band Spice Girls? Once again we see just how creative Aries—either male or female—can be.

As Aries is a moveable sign, this is why Victoria enjoys travelling immensely. She is constantly on the go with her famous husband David Beckham, and continues to strut the world stage and attract the attention of the paparazzi across the globe. It doesn't matter where Victoria appears in her travels, there's never a shortage of attention for her personal or professional exploits.

Some Aries-born individuals are so highly strung and active that they need to be careful not to burn too many kilojoules. This has been a point of contention and debate in the media over many years, which is why Victoria has been accused of having some sort of eating disorder. Whether or not that is true, you will find that the high metabolic rate of Aries natives is the primary reason for them not being able to maintain their weight. All that go-go-go lifestyle is a perfect way to burn up kilojoules.

Although she leads a glamorous lifestyle, it's quite a well-known fact that Victoria also takes tremendous pride in her family and, in particular, her children. This is another aspect of the Aries personality that is sometimes overlooked. Family is always in the back of their minds, even though they pursue numerous activities. Aries do indeed love and look after the welfare of their families.

Both Victoria and Quentin can look forward to some interesting times throughout 2012, because Venus, the planet of friendship, love and financial benefits, activates their profit sector as the year commences.

Having the added assistance of Uranus supercharging the loving Venus means they will be fulfilled in their desires, which could happen rather suddenly as the year commences. Friends will be a source of pleasure and profit for them.

However, August and September will be important turning points for both of these celebrities in their relationships, and they must not bury their heads in their work lest their love lives suffer.

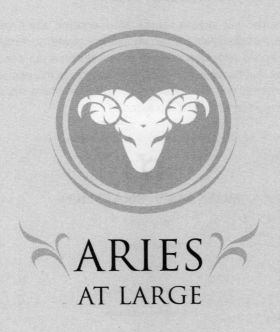

ARIES
AT LARGE

THE WORLD'S A STAGE AND MOST OF US ARE DESPERATELY UNREHEARSED.

Sean O'Casey

✄ ARIES MAN ✄

Aries men cut striking figures. Mars endows any Aries male, including you, with an abundance of vitality, sense of purpose and unadulterated charm. However, let's not forget that the aggressive and fiery aspects of this planet sometimes get the upper hand, which is where Aries men are sometimes misunderstood.

♂

ARIES MAN: SNAPSHOT

Strong willed

Physically vital

Arrogant

Great leadership qualities

Formidable competitor

Your ruling planet Mars is the Planet of War, so Aries men are never scared to stand up for a principle and go into battle to protect the people they love and cherish. You never back down, even if confronted by someone who may in fact be more powerful than or superior to you. You are courageous even in the face of danger or death.

As a natural-born leader, you rise to the top of your profession in a short time. This is not only because you like to be the best at what you do, but because you have an element of impatience in waiting around for the good things in life. You tend to push your way through if you can't get things going your way, in a reasonably short amount of time. Once you are at the top, you expect full allegiance from those around you, and reciprocate loyalty by helping those less capable than you are to achieve their ambitions as well.

Your sexual energies are very powerful, and you need people who can accommodate this high level of energy and, at times, demanding need. The relationship section later on will further explain some specific areas and compatibility ratings with star signs who will give you greater insight into this part of your nature. The bottom line is that you have a high sex drive that needs to be fulfilled, or it can turn into frustration, with devastating consequences for those around you. This is why it is so important for you, Aries, to take your time in selecting the right partners—not just sexual, but in business as well—who follow your lines of thought in a harmonious way, giving you ample scope to express these energies.

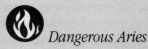

Dangerous Aries

It's a well-known fact that when Aries is pushed to the limit, or cornered in a fight or flight situation, the instinctive response of the endangered Aries male is to fight. Unfortunately, in the less-evolved person from this star sign, a lack of self-control can produce outbursts of emotion and physical violence, with ruthless and sometimes unpredictable consequences. In the higher-evolved type, this physical and retaliatory attitude may not be as prevalent as in the lower types, but the Aries male will nevertheless want to win in any circumstance.

You call a spade a spade even if it hurts other people's feelings. This doesn't particularly bother you. You hate having the residue of the past hanging around because there was some sort of misunderstanding about what you, they, or some third party meant. There's never any ambiguity in the way you communicate your ideas, and your bluntness is often not appreciated. But you'd agree that everyone will always know where they stand with you. There will never be any confusion about that. You may lose a few friends on the way, but that's a sacrifice you're prepared to make in your search for a transparent and integral life.

You are tenacious in going for your objectives and never stop until you have achieved them. You're relentless in pursuing your goals and will sometimes be callous in crushing your opponents—again using the Martian powers of your ruling planet to overtake any competitor, without taking any prisoners. Your adversaries should be warned about this personality streak within you.

Having said that, the softer, more sensitive and caring side of Aries men is often overlooked. I guess it's my job as your astrologer to remind you and others that there *is* a gentle side to Aries and, once that aspect of your character is revealed, people will have a completely different opinion of you. By the same token, you will be reluctant to show this part of your nature, because you never want to be perceived as exhibiting any sort of weakness. You feel this can be misconstrued by others and that you will be taken advantage of.

Be careful not to fall victim to your own ego. You may surround yourself with people who don't have the drive, ambition and self-respect that you do. If that's the case, you'll do yourself a great disservice. There's an old saying that goes, 'If you hang around a cripple long enough, you'll develop a limp'. Surround yourself with people who are *more* powerful than you, so you can lift yourself up to an even higher standard in your life. This is the secret of even greater successes for you, Aries.

⚹ ARIES WOMAN ⚹

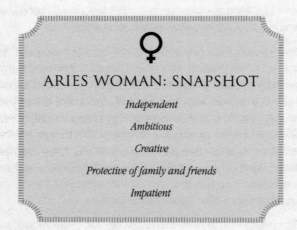

Your elegant, attractive physique and fiery eyes don't immediately reveal the intensity of your personality. Of course, everyone knows you're a woman on a mission by the speed of your speech, actions and mannerisms. This is your way of saying, 'Hey, you'd better pay attention to what I have to say now!' And indeed you will gain all the interest you want this way.

Elle Macpherson, the famous model and fashion designer, is a perfect example of a career-minded Aries girl, with her sleek, attractive physique and larger-than-life ambitions. Aries always wants to be first and women born under this sign are no exception.

You're an extraordinarily creative person and have the ability to come up with the goods under pressure. If you want anything done, give it to an Aries woman. People are completely flabbergasted at not only how quickly you can get something done, but how professionally you do it as well. However, you need to slow down as some Aries women tend to live on their nerves.

You have strong opinions and are sometimes seen as too black and white by people. It's not that you don't listen to others' opinions, it's just that you have a sense you're right, and what's so annoying to others is that you usually are! You're not the sort of person to get bored easily, because generally you have 101 things on the go at once. It's because of this that the Aries woman is usually successful, can assume responsible positions and is well-respected.

Friends feel overpowered by you because your enthusiasm and passion for life is so much more intense than theirs. Try to tone it down for those who haven't yet developed the same level of confidence as you.

Those in your life always know where they stand because of your honesty. Integrity is the key word for the Aries woman, so while people don't always like you they trust your words implicitly. If you say you'll do something, you'll do it, on time. And, speaking of getting the job done on time, you must learn to curb your impatience when things aren't happening as quickly as you'd like, or in the way you'd like them to.

Learn to set yourself realistic timelines so that you can get everything done without stress. Sometimes it seems as if everyone else is moving way too slowly, but actually it's you, Aries, who tends to move at lightning speed compared to others.

You'll be successful in life due to your highly ambitious nature and, even if you choose to be a homemaker, tending to your husband and children, this too will not be taken lightly, as you want to be the best at whatever you attempt. You are skilful and are considered an ace mother and homemaker.

To offset some of the tension you experience under your star sign, physical exercise is essential not only to help you look and feel good physically, but to calm your mind and emotions, and help you direct that effervescent energy of yours. You lead a hard and fast lifestyle, so working out is the best way to decompress.

Your friendships can be rocky, especially if you team up with characters who are just as headstrong as you. You'll need to make compromises as you hate taking a backseat in any relationship.

You love luxury and enjoying the good things in life. Strong colours, especially red, maroon and pink, will make you feel great. Being an Aries woman is a statement in itself.

✕ ARIES CHILD ✕

The first word that comes to mind when describing your little Aries child is demanding. Demanding, for sure. But other words that could equally describe them include curious, warm, lovable and energetic. These descriptions will more than compensate for the challenging test of your parental skills in raising these little rascals into fine, well-adjusted adults.

Most of the time your vibrant little ram will keep you on your toes from dawn till dusk—possibly even through to midnight. (Make that from midnight to dawn as well!) These kids are indeed highly charged bundles of energy which, if not managed, will cause them to get out of hand, create mischief, and possibly even become injury prone. They may even occasionally run into brick walls due to their restlessness. Be prepared for the regular bumps, bruises, and even the odd stitch here and there due to this characteristic. It's not a bad idea to have a first-aid kit on hand.

Curious Aries

Demanding Aries children are curious beings. Your Aries child is persistently on the lookout for the how, why and where of this world. Impatient in their incessant demands upon you, sooner or later you'll have to ask yourself who's actually running the show: you or them? You'll need to set down strict guidelines early in their lives to make sure they don't get the upper hand. You know that Aries do like to be in charge, and this goes for the youngsters of this star sign as well.

There's no doubting, however, that children born under this star sign are incredibly loving and caring and, as they grow older, you'll feel an endearing quality about them that supersedes the challenges of rearing them (or possibly even cursing them when you just can't seem to contain them!). But the Aries child, both male and female, is one of the most demonstrative and affectionate. You'll get your daily round of cuddles, alternating with a blatant disregard for what you ask them to do. This is definitely a rollercoaster ride for any parent.

Understand clearly that your competitive Aries child needs sport, plenty of outdoor activities and fresh air, coupled with a balanced diet and adequate rest. They will excel in any sort of sport in which they can prove their stamina, strength and desire to win. You must, by the same token, teach them the art of good sportsmanship, because they hate to lose.

You'll be surprised at the rich imagination with which Aries children are endowed. Reading them stories triggers their imagination and makes them feel as if they're actually living the story as you read to them. In their quest to reach their ideals, be sure to draw a line in the sand when they become pushy, or try to overtake their peers by being bossy. The art of sharing power is one of the best lessons you can teach them as a parent.

✂ ARIES LOVER ✂

❝ I NEED AT LEAST THREE WHOLE MINUTES TO MAKE LOVE TO YOU, SAYS ARIES, WHEN AROUSED. ❞

Cᴏ

Dull or inactive lovers need not apply for a relationship with Aries. The fact of the matter is that becoming romantically involved with someone born under your star sign is a full-time commitment, requiring attention, physical energy and creative reciprocation. There's no escaping indirection with an Aries lover.

However, if your partner is able to give 100 per cent to a relationship, they can expect a life of passion, excitement and affection. You will actively go out of your way to make life fun and fulfilling in every possible way. If other star signs are reading this, we should mention that if they are in a relationship with you they are indeed lucky, because you will be prepared to offer a great deal of variety when it comes to the relationship.

Because Mars rules your personality, and is the driving force behind your birth sign, it stands to reason that sex is of primary importance in your relationships. If the words dull and inactive describe your lover in the bedroom, rest assured the relationship will not go very far at all. You need a creative lover between the sheets, someone who will provide for each and every one of your sensual needs, and explore the fantasies you aspire to. If you find someone fitting this description, this will go a long way towards ensuring a satisfactory experience.

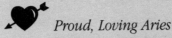

Proud, Loving Aries

Aries love to feel that they can showcase the person they love to the world, and take great pride in their relationships. You'll attract many partners in your life due to the combined influence of Mars and Venus, and will be selective in your choice of 'The One'. You need to prove your prowess, especially if you are a man born under this sign.

Being born under Aries means you are quick off the mark when it comes to involving yourself with new partners. Particularly in the early part of your life, you like to 'play the field' and explore what's on offer. You may sometimes be accused of being shallow or commitment-phobic. That's not altogether true, because you like to filter out what's not going to work, and get to the point as quickly as possible. At least you don't keep people tethered to a relationship when you know it isn't going to amount to much.

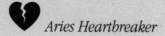

Aries Heartbreaker

Some of the broken hearts who have come and gone shouldn't feel too bad, because at least you were totally honest with them.

And that brings us to the aspect of Aries' ruthless honesty. As Jack Nicholson said to Tom Cruise in the movie *A Few Good Men*, 'You can't handle the truth!' This is the case for most of the other star sign personalities who deal with Aries in a relationship. In fact, Jack Nicholson's attitude in that scene depicts fairly accurately the manner in which the truth is delivered by an Aries. They are blunt and unforgiving. And it's true: most thin-skinned individuals will not be able to handle what Aries have to say all that well.

In marriage, Aries, you make an ideal partner, always putting your family and loved ones above everything else. Sometimes this is hard for others to see because you spend considerable time away from them earning money to acquire the best things in life, but only ever doing it as a means of satisfying them and proving that you have their interests at heart. You are protective and will never allow anyone to harm the ones you love, or step over the line of what you consider your territory.

⊱ ARIES FRIEND ⊱

You are one of the most loyal friends a person could hope to have. Even though people often accuse you of being self-centred and sometimes neglectful of your family and friends, when it comes to the crunch you do indeed 'put your money where your mouth is' and demonstrate your loyalty to those who need you. You may have an unusual way of showing it, which is part of your independent nature, but your loyalty would never be questioned if others didn't judge you too soon or too superficially.

You are extremely active in your social life and passionate about all your social engagements. You like to get involved socially and inject a great deal of energy—not just as a participant, but as an initiator—into functions, parties and other get-togethers of family and friends. Friends often ask you from where you get your vitality. It's an inbuilt thing with you, probably genetic. One thing is sure, however: you have the sort of humour and vitality that is infectious, and those around you can't help but feel uplifted by your presence.

A friendship with Aries is warm and on the level. You expect absolute loyalty in friendship and in return extend a loving and strong hand. But people should never expect you to turn a blind eye when you realise they have done something wrong. It doesn't work like that with you. You need to tell them exactly how you feel, and sometimes the words that come out of your mouth may not be all that pleasant or what your peers want to hear. But rest assured that your concern comes from a space of love and respect. By the same token, you would expect your friends to reciprocate the same honesty, wouldn't you, Aries?

Arians sometimes like to look for diverse kinds of friends, and for you, just as much as anyone, that is the spice of life. Boredom is one of the traits you can't tolerate, either in your own life or in another person's character. Apathy, laziness—either physically or emotionally—creates rifts between you and those you may even have known for years. They must lift their ball game if they are going to maintain a relationship with you. In order to grab hold of your attention, people should be exciting and surprising on a regular basis. Adventurous people attract you.

You have a tendency to get upset easily. This is one personality trait you should work on to improve the quality of your relationships. If you learn to curb your impatience, arrogance and need to dominate others, your friendships will prosper and life will be much happier.

✂ ARIES ENEMY ✂

❝ 'OUCH! DID SOMEONE JUST CUT OFF MY HEAD WITH A RAZOR-SHARP SWORD WITHOUT MY KNOWING IT?' ASKED AN ENEMY OF ARIES. 'UM, YES, BUT I HAVEN'T QUITE FINISHED WITH YOU YET', REPLIED ARIES. ❞

∽

My strong recommendation for a would-be enemy of Aries is to think twice before engaging in war with them. Their namesake is, after all, a derivative of the warring planet Mars, and this endows them with ferocity, competitive instincts, an insatiable desire to win (and to be right), and never to stop until the job is done.

It's far better to have Aries as an ally, even if you don't particularly like them. Keep them at arm's distance I say, and if it's you, Aries, reading this, my suggestion is to develop a little more mercy with your opponents. While writing this I can't help but recall the Roman gladiator fights, and how ruthless the champions must have been when inflicting their final wounds on their helpless competitors.

You also need to be less impulsive in jumping to conclusions. You have a tendency to think the worst before getting all your facts straight. By accusing others of wrongdoing you alienate even close friends and it becomes difficult to make amends once you've demolished someone.

ARIES
AT HOME

THE TRAGEDY OF LIFE IS WHAT DIES
INSIDE A MAN WHILE HE LIVES.

Albert Einstein

❧ HOME FRONT ❧

The Aries character loves being at home *when* they are at home. For the most part, Aries, you are always on the go, and this is due to your star sign being a common or *moveable* zodiac sign. You generally don't enjoy staying still and you look for daily excitement. You do, however, very much need to have a stable base from which to co-ordinate many of your activities.

If you are a married Aries, returning home each afternoon to your family will be a source of relaxation, so this is an excellent way to unwind and recover your physical and creative energies at the end of a hard-working day.

A barbeque on weekends at home will find you behind the grill, marinating the meat and preparing the food for guests, and then serving everyone present. You are a great entertainer and enjoy the company of friends, telling jokes and sharing stories, as well as a bottle of the finest wine. These get-togethers are usually boisterous, interactive, and always fun.

Houseproud Aries

Aries are always active, making their houses look great. You want a comfortable but exciting environment in which to entertain and relax. Bold colours are your style because you want your house to be an extension and expression of your powerful and charming personality. Aries needs plenty of room for independent space, and time for their own exploits.

A fast-paced, city mode of living is the type of lifestyle you prefer; a home with loads of space, large rooms and, if possible, a fancy, attractive façade as the entrance to your domain.

Because the ruling colour of Aries is red, the best colours for your interior decor come from the autumn shades, with dashes of yellow, orange and other striking contrasts. This makes you feel alive. You want your house to make a statement about who you are.

Straight lines without embellishment suit your taste in furnishings, with room to play. You hate feeling cramped, and if you live in a smaller apartment without enough space to spread your wings to fly, this will start to play out on your moods, creating a negative reaction within you. Bright colours lift your spirits and make you feel as if you are in your element.

You love the latest gadgets like a big LCD television, efficient remote controls, a slick CD player and a good collection of CDs. These act as a background to your exciting lifestyle when you do relax. Fire is your element, so when you sit down and take it easy, particularly in the cold months, a fireplace with warm, red flames is a perfect ingredient for you to unwind and enjoy a little time out. But mark this down in your diary or it may not happen!

 Warning! Warning!

If you are an Aries, *never* live in a house without adequate space. You need plenty of it, and if you don't have it, you will surely explode from frustration.

KARMA, LUCK AND MEDITATION

Aries are generally lucky through their own efforts and exertion, due to the fact that Mars is self-initiatory. In other words, you don't need to rely on others for your success. You do, however, have the auspicious Jupiter ruling your zone of past karma and good fortune. As a result of this, even just a little effort on your part will result in exceptionally good karmic reactions in this life. You also have a considerable stock of good karma from actions in your previous existence, if we are to believe the doctrine of karma.

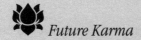

Future Karma

Your future karma and what is likely to happen in this life is ruled by Leo and the Sun. This again is a lucky omen and indicates a bright future, with your speculations and good gut instincts resulting in positive actions and overall good karma.

'I Am' is your most notable phrase. Try to become more aware of yourself, your reactions towards others and their reactions to you. This is the best way to improve your relationships, find peace of mind, and achieve even greater happiness in your life.

Mondays, Sundays, Tuesdays and Thursdays are lucky

for spiritual pursuits and self-development. Spend some time daily slowing your pace to achieve happiness, which will in turn generate better luck for you.

Lucky Days
Your luckiest days are Monday, Tuesday, Thursday and Sunday.

Lucky Numbers
Lucky numbers for Aries include the following. You may wish to experiment with these in lotteries and other games of chance:

9, 18, 27, 36, 45, 54

1, 10, 19, 28, 37, 46

3, 12, 21, 30, 48, 57

Destiny Years
The most significant years in your life are likely to be 9, 18, 27, 36, 45, 54, 63, 72 and 81.

HEALTH, WELLBEING ❧ AND DIET ❧

Those born under Aries should try not to think too much about health issues. There are two reasons for this. The first has more to do with the fact that you are a positive person. You like to believe you are beyond sickness and are resilient to anything holding you back from your normal routine.

The second is the fact that the Aries is one of the most powerful and enduring signs, resulting in good health, powerful stamina and also great longevity. When and if some sort of illness occurs, it's amazing how quickly you can lift yourself up and get better. Physical problems don't normally keep you down for long.

Aries rules the head, therefore anything to do with this region of anatomy will usually be the constitutionally weak part of your star sign. Headaches, earaches and, occasionally, eyesight issues may become a problem, particularly later in life.

Because you play and work hard, moderate your lifestyle, rest adequately and eat well. Don't eat on the run, and spend some time enjoying your meals in a relaxed atmosphere. Don't skimp on meals.

Because you love spices and hot foods, be careful not to overstimulate your body and your mind. You have enough of the Aries fire already, so don't add more fuel to it! This will dry out your body and create problems with your skin, including eczema, psoriasis and other hard-to-manage skin conditions.

It's not a bad idea to keep up your vitamin intake and concentrate on flaxseed oil and other antioxidants that will prevent the ageing of your skin. Carry a bottle of water with you to hydrate yourself, and this will go a long way in preventing the drying and flaking of your skin.

Focus on mixing your meat intake with a copious supply of green, leafy vegetables. Raw foods are rich in nutrients and minerals, and will also support your stamina. Avoid coffee, tea, nicotine and alcohol, which overstimulate you.

✕ FINANCE FINESSE ✕

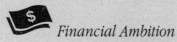

Financial Ambition

Although sometimes you are rather reckless with money, others aren't aware that you have a strong need for financial security, borne out by Venus and Taurus being the rulers of your financial sector. Because of this, you will work with indomitable dedication towards fulfilling your ambitions and earning as much money as you can, even if success and affluence aren't forthcoming too quickly.

Aquarius is the ruler of your profitability sector, and this indicates your unique ability to think outside the square and earn money in ways people may not necessarily consider. You are ingenious, progressive and also tenacious in achieving financial stability.

You must be careful not to be overly generous with your money, and put aside a little each week for a rainy day. Sometimes you are overconfident about how much you have and your capacity to repay a debt. Due to this you may end up with huge financial commitments and, thereafter, an incredibly huge workload trying to pay it back. Temper your impatient and restless attitude towards achieving things quickly. This way, you will avoid putting yourself under undue financial pressure.

ARIES

AT WORK

DOUBT IS NOT A PLEASANT
CONDITION, BUT CERTAINTY IS AN
ABSURD ONE.

Voltaire

✄ ARIES CAREER ✄

IDEAL PROFESSIONS

Emergency personnel—triage nurse, fireman, search and rescue

Armed services personnel

Policewoman/man or law enforcement officer

Independent business owner

Butcher

Salesperson

Travel agent

Sportsperson or sports-accessories retailer

Work is a therapeutic activity for you. Whether you're a corporate animal or at home raising a family, you need to feel productive and useful in society.

You will pursue a profession that gives you variety and change. Anything to do with sports, sales or an entrepreneurial line of work is a pretty good choice for you. You're very sociable and you like the idea of interacting with groups of people in working situations.

Careers in which you're able to use your hands can also give you a great deal of satisfaction, because you are manually quite dexterous.

You are a person of great initiative and inspire those with whom you work. You make a great boss but at times you are a little demanding. Exercise more patience and understanding to those not as experienced or skilful as you are.

Generally, you'll be successful in your work, but try to curb your impatience and your successes will be that much sweeter.

 Mars: God of War

Your ruling planet Mars is the God of War. What does this mean to you professionally? You need to be Number 1 in all your professional activities. Mars is daring, warlike and courageous. You can attempt a career path that is unique, challenging and ambitious. You will tread an unbeaten path and, where others fail, you will succeed.

You are a fine leader and others look up to you. At times you are aggressive in wanting things done yesterday. Curb your impatience and irritability and the world will be your oyster.

 Saturn

Your career ruler, Saturn, helps focus your attention on the task at hand, and makes you tenacious about achieving your career goals. Although you have a tendency to get across the finish line quickly, you have a long-term patience that will leave others for dead when it comes to gaining your objectives.

⚤ ARIES BOSS ⚤

The synonym for boss is Aries. You are a capable boss but expect hard work, diligence and loyalty from your employees. In a position of authority, you are dynamic in the execution of your professional duties. You can't stand sloth or inactivity of any sort, and quickly weed out anyone who is bringing down the morale of the team. Laziness will not be tolerated by you, as you yourself are an extremely hard-working individual and are not afraid to get your hands dirty, so to speak.

Employees whom you hire will never quite know what any day will bring, because intensity is one of the key words that best describes your interaction with them. By the same token, you create an environment that inspires excitement, the promise of great rewards, hard work and a sense of fun.

Willpower seems to be another strong feature associated with your Aries birth. Determination, independence and a clear focus on what you wish to achieve make you successful at whatever you set your mind to. But you will not tolerate disloyalty of any sort because you believe your goodwill should be reciprocated by those to whom you extend generosity. If employees cross you, they'll have to deal with your wrath.

You are physically strong and tend to overwork. You must be careful not to transpose this work ethic on those less capable. Improve your skills as an employer. It's not a bad idea to occasionally take time to sit with your employees and talk about their personal situations, abilities and limitations. You want to push them beyond their limits and bring out their best.

Your dynamic personality is sometimes daunting to employees, but by the same token, you are respected for your sincerity and desire to create the best for those who work for and with you. However, it's best if none of your underlings outshine you, because your ego is something that doesn't take too kindly to not being the centre of attention.

You have an unusual approach to hiring new employees in that you tend to view them independent of their past history of good or bad reports. You use their curriculum vitae as an initial means of getting a clear picture, but are a free thinker and make decisions based upon your own insights. You listen to the advice of others, but don't always act on that advice.

⊱ ARIES EMPLOYEE ⊰

 Enthusiastic Employee

What will impress any employer in an interview with a would-be Aries employee is the sheer enthusiasm they bring to the table. He or she might possibly think that they are not quite qualified enough, but Aries' vivacious and positive attitude will more than compensate for some of their shortcomings. For this reason, employers probably won't have any hesitation in hiring the Ram on the spot.

You must understand that, as an Aries, your primary requirement is freedom and creative latitude. Irrespective of the position you're hired for, as long as these two key ingredients are a part of your work brief, your boss will be satisfied with the eventual results.

ANYTHING BUT BORING

You mustn't be constricted by a dull routine, or too much of a traditional deadline mentality. You buck at this.

You will get the work done as long as you are given enough space and incentive to make you work hard, which you love doing. If your employer doesn't get this right, you will simply build up considerable resentment and create problems for co-workers, yourself and possibly even your boss.

As an Aries employee you are determined, committed and energetic in meeting your goals, but you mustn't be pushed too hard, even if employers don't see the results in the first instance. You have your own methods of achieving results and should be trusted on this. If you are respected by your employer, they will receive the same respect in return.

The old saying, 'Pay peanuts and you'll get monkeys', is true, especially of you, Aries. I'm not saying that you are in any way a monkey, because you work so hard at quite the opposite. But if what's on offer is a pittance, you'll feel less than enthusiastic about doing your best. You'll need to be paid handsomely to work at full steam. If you are paid well, your employer will be more than satisfied with what you offer.

Ladder of Success

Because of your tenacity and commitment to hard work, it doesn't worry you too much to start on the lowest rung of the ladder, as long as you can see a growth path containing the promise of bigger and better things to come.

Money is not the main reason you work; for you, it's more to do with getting paid what you are worth—more to do with your ego and status. Your boss should never make the mistake of giving credit to someone else for your work. If that happens, you are likely to walk out at the drop of a hat, leaving your manager high and dry. Pride is a very strong component of an Aries-born individual. You exhibit this in your work.

PROFESSIONAL RELATIONSHIPS: BEST AND WORST

BEST PAIRING: ARIES AND SAGITTARIUS

Both you and Sagittarius respect and appreciate each other's drive and ambition to achieve a common goal. This is why, as business partners, you are likely to get on quite well. The common fire element makes you both high-spirited and positive about what you can achieve in your business life together.

One thing that is extremely important in any professional relationship is the issue of trust, and with your Sagittarian partner, you can certainly trust them to get the job done. They may, however, have a tendency to be a little scattered. If, in your busy schedule, you find this difficult to monitor, it could be a problem with you both spreading yourselves too thinly.

It's essential at the outset that you both agree on what your parameters and objectives are in the commercial enterprise, and at the same time set yourselves clear guidelines for the work you will both do, individually and collectively.

Neither of you are prepared to settle for second best.

Worn out, traditional approaches to making money seem quite boring, which is another wonderful thing about teaming up with a Sagittarian. They agree that it's quite okay to step outside the normal rules of thinking to create something refreshingly new and exciting for the marketplace.

Because your Sagittarian business partner likes to travel, it's a great idea to give them scope to do so. They have the ability to draw in people from all walks of life and cultures, to create brand new markets that you yourself may not have considered.

Sagittarians are great storytellers, but may sometimes overembellish their anecdotes, which is why you'll need to maintain a watchful eye to keep their sales pitches for your company or product from bordering on inaccuracies that could be misconstrued as dishonest. The two of you want to maintain as much integrity as possible to create a successful enterprise.

Finally, because you are so busy trying to meet your own deadlines, you sometimes forget that Sagittarius needs time and attention to share opinions with you. Take a little time to acknowledge them and your business should prosper.

WORST PAIRING:
ARIES AND CAPRICORN

Both you and Capricorn are hard-working and ambitious. However, it's a complicated scenario if you decide to team up with a Capricorn for the purposes of setting up a business, because you are both extremely independent individuals. Bringing your energies together as a working team will end up creating a battle of wills between you, the Ram, and Capricorn, the Goat.

The problem is that Capricorn, to your way of thinking, is way too preoccupied with the finer details of the organisation, and a meticulous adherence to its structure and schedule that borders on the extreme. Your preference in any department of life—and in particular, your professional life—is to have a reasonable degree of scope to express yourself independently and spontaneously from moment to moment. Capricorn will try to constrain this creative side of your personality, with disastrous results.

Both of you are active and highly motivated to achieve success, but you, Aries, will always come across as way too egotistical to Capricorn. Capricorn wants to change you, to mould you into something that is too traditional for your liking. My own experience tells me, from dealing with Aries individuals, that the worst thing you can do with this star sign is force them to do something they do not want to do. If you contradict their opinions, all hell will break loose. Capricorns reading this and thinking of getting into business with Aries would do well to reconsider, or at least prepare to loosen up a little and do things the Arian way.

When it comes to trying to motivate Capricorn, when you feel that rush of enthusiasm and excitement that comes from simply being Aries, you'll be greatly let down, receiving what could be considered a most underwhelming response from them. This will dampen the fire of your aspiration. Remember, although you're both moveable and active zodiac signs, Capricorn is earth and you are fire. Fire does not function well with this element as its counterpart. If you want to put out a fire, just throw some dirt on it. I'm sure you get my point.

There may be some differences in the way both of you function, depending on who is the employer and who is the employee. It would be disastrous for you if Capricorn was the boss. You would feel so inhibited and constrained that you might just walk out without a word. On the other hand, although you have your work cut out for you trying to push Capricorn out of their zone of cold comfort, you are not averse to working hard to motivate Capricorn. Therefore, it would probably be better for you, Aries, to motivate them from the position of leader.

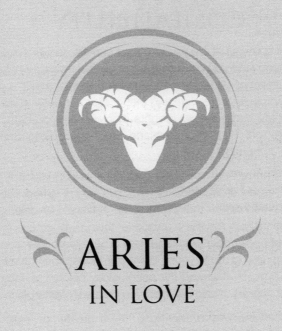

ARIES

IN LOVE

ALL THE PASSIONS MAKE US COMMIT
FAULTS; LOVE MAKES US COMMIT
THE MOST RIDICULOUS ONES.

François de La Rochefoucauld

ROMANTIC
⚹ COMPATIBILITY ⚹

How compatible are you with your current partner, lover or friend? Did you know that astrology can reveal a whole new level of understanding between people, simply by looking at their star sign and that of their partner? I'd like to share some special insights that will help you better appreciate your strengths and challenges using Sun sign compatibility.

The Sun reflects your drive, willpower and personality. The essential qualities of two star signs blend like two pure colours that produce an entirely new colour. Relationships, similarly, produce their own emotional colours when two people interact. The following section is a general guide to your romantic prospects with others and how, by knowing the astrological 'colour' of each other, the art of love can help you create a masterpiece.

Each of the twelve star signs has a greater or lesser affinity with the others. The two quick-reference tables will show you who's hot and who's not as far as your relationships are concerned.

The Star Sign Compatibility table rates your chance as a percentage of general compatibility, while the Horoscope Compatibility table summarises the reasons why. The results of each star sign combination are also listed.

When reading I ask you to remember that no two star signs are ever totally incompatible. With effort and compromise, even the most difficult astrological matches can work. Don't close your mind to the full range of life's possibilities! Learning about each other and ourselves is the most important facet of astrology.

Good luck in your search for love, and may the stars shine upon you in 2012!

STAR SIGN COMPATIBILITY
FOR LOVE AND FRIENDSHIP
(PERCENTAGES)

	Aries	Taurus	Gemini	Cancer	Leo	Virgo	Libra	Scorpio	Sagittarius	Capricorn	Aquarius	Pisces
Aries	60	65	65	65	90	45	70	80	90	50	55	65
Taurus	60	70	70	80	70	90	75	85	50	95	80	85
Gemini	70	70	75	60	80	75	90	60	75	50	90	50
Cancer	65	80	60	75	70	75	60	95	55	45	70	90
Leo	90	70	80	70	85	75	65	75	95	45	70	75
Virgo	45	90	75	75	75	70	80	85	70	95	50	70
Libra	70	75	90	60	65	80	80	85	80	85	95	50
Scorpio	80	85	60	95	75	85	85	90	80	65	60	95
Sagittarius	90	50	75	55	95	70	80	85	85	55	60	75
Capricorn	50	95	50	45	45	95	85	65	55	85	70	85
Aquarius	55	80	90	70	70	50	95	60	60	70	80	55
Pisces	65	85	50	90	75	70	50	95	75	85	55	80

In the compatibility table above please note that some compatibilities have seemingly contradictory ratings. Why you ask? Well, remember that no two people experience the relationship in exactly the same way. For one person a relationship may be more advantageous, more supportive than for the other. Sometimes one gains more than the other partner and therefore the compatibility rating will be higher for them.

HOROSCOPE COMPATIBILITY FOR ARIES

Aries with		Romance/Sexual
Aries		Explosive and passionate affair, but may not last
Taurus		Loving and sensual combination
Gemini		Better friends than lovers, but may have a quick love affair
Cancer		Moody and emotionally turbulent relationship
Leo		Great love match and mutually supportive

Friendship	Professional
✔ Good friends, but may disagree often	✘ Need to determine who will be boss
✔ Enjoy hanging out, but stubborn Taurus may not be adventurous enough	✔ Good financial match
✔ Great communication, intellectually stimulating	✔ You are of great assistance to Gemini and assist their ambitions
✘ You irritate Cancer because they don't think you are sensitive enough—show your softer side	✘ Too domineering for Cancer
✔ Bosom buddies	✔ Playful and creative workmates

Aries with		Romance/Sexual
Virgo		Their incessant need for hygiene as part of their lovemaking ritual is weird to you
Libra		Passionate and intense romantic affair, but a rollercoaster ride for the most part
Scorpio		Intense, but ego clashes are likely; great lovemaking
Sagittarius		Excellent match between the sheets; physically fulfilling
Capricorn		Too cold and calculating for you
Aquarius		Quirky match and may enjoy a fling
Pisces		Pisces will provide you compassionate love, but this may not be enough

Friendship	Professional
✘ Terrible combination—finicky Virgo drives you nuts	✔ They will serve you well and you respect their dedication professionally
✘ Blows hot and cold—Libra is too indecisive for you	✔ You challenge each other a lot; Libra is creative and you're the driver (get rid of the whip, though)
✔ Great friends, but also intellectually challenging	✔ Formidable combo that can achieve success
✔ Warm, exciting match; adventurous combo	✔ Work well together, but draw the line between work and play
✔ May balance each other, but Capricorn is also very conservative	✔ Work well together, but you are too quick for slow-plodding Capricorn
✔ Good friends	✔ Inventive Aquarius is profitable for you
✔ Spiritually enlightening friendship	✘ Pisces slows you down and may cost you financially in the end

ARIES
PARTNERSHIPS

Aries + Aries

The great thing about the two of you is that you will encourage each other in work and social areas. However, too much individual independence may create rifts between you, giving rise to possessiveness. You have to keep the flames of love alive with continual effort.

Aries + Taurus

Your impulsive financial nature will threaten the more conservative and security conscious Taurus. You will need to restrain yourself and accommodate the grounded Taurus character. If you can be humble enough to listen to the practical advice of your bullish friend, Taurus will give you the support you need.

Aries + Gemini

Gemini stimulates your imagination and this is useful for you to develop your personality. Sexually, you feel comfortable with each other, as your ruling planets are very friendly. You'll be attracted to Gemini's curious and inventive mind. They love your sensuality while you adore their minds.

Aries + Cancer

If Cancer is capable and willing to give you the much-desired freedom you require, this partnership can quite likely work. You need variety in love, however, and Cancer might be a little too staid, if not boring, on a long-term basis.

 Aries + Leo

You have a very powerful sexual connection with Leo, but remember to take things slow and easy. It will take a little time for the two of you to deepen your affection for each other beyond the initial explosion of your meeting. Once that happens, you may be able to find a lasting relationship. You are both quite stubborn in your opinions.

 Aries + Virgo

The cool, critical and perfection-loving Virgo is a completely different kettle of fish to you, Aries. In fact, Virgo is so different that you may feel completely at odds with them, even irritated. You could also find yourself getting pretty angry with their perfectionist attitude.

Aries + Libra

In the bedroom, your energies will find an exciting union, but on other levels, they may not be quite as compatible. Both your emotional and sexual rapport will be strong, and your initial meeting could have all the hallmarks of an instinctive sexual urge.

 Aries + Scorpio

Without doubt Scorpio will take your breath away! Their power is quite likely beyond any you've experienced before. In the realm of relationships, this is a unique and intense combination. It is vital from the outset. But…can you handle it?

 Aries + Sagittarius

This combination is one of great joy and playfulness. There's a raw innocence in your coming together with a Sagittarian. The planets ruling your star signs are very friendly and ensure an expansive relationship for the two of you.

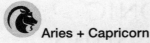

Aries + Capricorn

This really is a pretty tough romantic combination, with the forecast being an uphill battle, Aries! Some astrologers might even say that this is one of the most *uncomfortable* matches in the zodiac!

Aries + Aquarius

Both of you are extremely independent individuals and need ample space in which to allow your personalities the freedom to grow. Based on respect for each other, a relationship between you would bring out the better qualities you both possess.

Aries + Pisces

Pisces will love you unconditionally, especially when it comes to fulfilling your ever-growing sensual appetites. They'll provide more than you're prepared to reciprocate. You mustn't take Pisces for granted if you plan a relationship with them.

PLATONIC RELATIONSHIPS: ❧ BEST AND WORST ❧

BEST PAIRING: ARIES AND AQUARIUS

The fact that Aquarius falls on the eleventh sign to Aries is an indication of the great friendship that occurs between these two signs of the zodiac. Mind you, there are some ancient systems of astrology that warn against the combination of Aquarius and Aries, because Aquarius can be rather fixed in their opinions, and Aries rather volatile due to the element of fire that dominates it.

Notwithstanding the above introduction to your rather complicated friendship, you will feel comfortable with Aquarius, who will stimulate your mind, and, of course, by being an air sign, will fan the fires of your intense passion. This is exactly how it should be with an Aries. However, when I speak of passion with an Aquarius, let me suggest that this is not necessarily the passion of sensual, physical action, so much as an intellectual camaraderie based upon mutual respect and understanding.

Aquarius is more involved with Aries in a general sense, according to the dictums of astrology. Aquarius is very much concerned with social interaction and other humanitarian pursuits that are designed to improve the group rather than just the individual. This is how you will learn from your Aquarius friend, Aries, so pay special attention to their mode of living and the lifestyle they employ. You will be fascinated by them and somewhat interested in adopting some of these elements for your own way of living. By doing so, your friendship with Aquarius will elevate your state of mind, your spiritual aspirations and your compassionate nature.

The eleventh sign to Aries is also concerned with profitability in a material sense. It will be through the combined efforts of Aquarius and Aries that some of your lifelong desires will be fulfilled on a practical level, not just an intellectual one. Working hard together affords you the opportunity to achieve something of worth together. But be careful that you don't overstep the boundaries of good taste, the limits to what is acceptable and not. You may want to push this friendship beyond what it is really meant to be, and that is when things may go terribly wrong. It is better to keep a friend than lose a friend.

WORST PAIRING:
ARIES AND VIRGO

Those born under the sign of Virgo are, to your way of thinking, very generous, particularly when it comes to advice! However, this is precisely why a friendship with Virgo is an extremely difficult thing if you are born under Aries. You would far prefer Virgo to be less generous with their critique of everything, from your personality traits to the way you do things, even when it comes to cleanliness. It's not that you are barbaric in your daily hygiene, but at times you prefer to hang loose, rather than be clinically scrubbed up before doing everything, like a surgeon at your local intensive-care unit.

It's never going to be easy to compromise with a Virgo, whether you have a professional, sexual or platonic relationship. They consider you to be too abrasive and opinionated in the way you come across. You find them all extremely sensitive, thin-skinned people, and incapable of hearing the truth in the rough and ready way you prefer to give it.

In some ways you find Virgo's sensitivity a form of weakness, and if you do, you are being a harsh judge of your Virgo friend. Virgo has some extraordinarily subtle strengths from which you could possibly learn. Perfection is not the exclusive property of Virgo, but they have made it quite a hobby, and the way in which they approach their work is something to behold. When applying this aspiration for perfection to their friendships—their emotional and mental connections—you find their need for perfection rather odd. In fact, this could be the cause of many arguments between you.

Astrologically, Aries and Virgo are in what is known as a 6–8 position. This is probably the worst pairing between star signs, which is why you and Virgo—if you have to deal with each other in a social context—need to accept that there will be many lessons for both of you to learn. I never say anything is impossible, but this friendship combination, if you want to call it that, comes pretty close.

SEXUAL RELATIONSHIPS: ✕ BEST AND WORST ✕

BEST PAIRING:
ARIES AND LEO

Leo is one of your best love matches in the zodiac as far as romantic relationships go. Leo, as with Aries, is a fire sign, and knows how to stimulate you. You feel as if you can relate to them without being overpowered by their exuberance and strong presence.

Leos are great fun and you love this about them. Leo is sexually satisfying to you, Aries. This is a near-perfect score of 10 between the sheets. You'll be fulfilled physically and emotionally, and you'll both understand each other's desires. There's an instinctive insight into each other's needs, and you'll be prepared to satisfy each other completely.

Leo individuals are passionate about their interests, and you must always take the time to acknowledge this in them if you want to improve your relationship. You must also learn that Leo is more opinionated and less adaptable in their opinions, although this doesn't mean they don't consider your perspective on certain topics.

You both tend to gravitate towards a common set of friends, which also helps your relationship. There's nothing worse than wanting to be with a certain group of people only to find out that your partner prefers a different clique. This can create rifts, but in this case, you and Leo will find agreement. You enjoy giving dinners and entertaining your friends at home.

Being strong willed and opinionated yourself means that you can come into conflict over certain topics at different times. The trick here, Aries, is to learn to be less egotistical and domineering in your views. If you can put aside your desire to be right, you will enjoy your friendship with Leo just that much more.

Leo is inspired by your drive and energy. The more they see of it, the more they want to get behind you and power you up to the max. Likewise, you have the ability to help your Leo lover achieve bigger and better things just by being yourself, Aries. Your mutual admiration is strong, and there is a common objective—and possibly even philosophical ideal—that you both share. In short, this is an excellent match, romantically and sexually.

WORST PAIRING:
ARIES AND CANCER

You might at first think that Cancer would be the perfect counterbalance to your fiery temperament because it is ruled by the element of water. But this just isn't the case. Of course, Cancer is a soft, sensitive and emotional type, which you may be drawn to initially as a means of soothing your rather intense nature. However, eventually you'll realise that the changeable moods of your Cancerian partner are not only incompatible with your own but are, without a doubt, a heavy weight on your shoulders.

You need to keep things moving, flowing and upbeat. The pendulum motion of the Cancerian personality is something that will drive you crazy. You'll feel bogged down trying to understand why they feel the way they do. To you, life is straightforward and uncomplicated, yet Cancer's response to your emotional needs is illogical and very time consuming. In the beginning you'll make concessions, but after a while you will be brutally retaliatory, and resent the smothering, mothering nature of the Crab.

NOT A PROMISING DESTINY

*In those moments, just when you feel Cancer is onside
and ready to support you in your vivacious push to
achieve something worthwhile for both of you, their
temperamental outbursts, sulking episodes and long,
drawn-out, teary, deep-and-meaningful discussions
will have you heading for the door. Cancer will, of
course, make a last ditch effort to salvage what is
probably not really a retrievable relationship. You'll see
this, but unfortunately Cancer will not.*

Passion is not exactly synchronous with both of your star signs. The way in which you love and wish to be loved is very different in the pairing of Aries with Cancer. Sexually you prefer playful, loud and sometimes experimental physicality, while Cancer is prone to be less outspoken about their needs. You might interpret this inaction as holding back, when in fact Cancers are simply more sensitive and, at times, reserved in expressing themselves, until they become fully acquainted with you. If you're already in a relationship with this watery sea creature and you wish to make a go of it, you'll need to be patient and take the time to understand them on their terms.

If you adapt yourself and employ some of your intuition to 'tune in' to Cancer's needs, they may find you a much-needed inspiration to lift them out of the emotional way they live their lives and relate to others. Once you coach them on how to express themselves spontaneously and not get too hung up on the trivia of life, you might indeed find they have more to offer than you first thought. But this could be an uphill battle and a long-term project for which your Aries impatience may not find the time.

QUIZ:
HAVE YOU FOUND
YOUR PERFECT
✂ MATCH? ✂

Do you dare take the following quiz to see just how good a lover you are? Remember, although the truth sometimes hurts, it's the only way to develop your relationship skills.

We are all searching for our soulmate: that idyllic romantic partner who will fulfil our wildest dreams of love and emotional security. Unfortunately, finding true love isn't easy. Sometimes, even when you are in a relationship, you can't help but wonder whether or not your partner is right for you. How can you possibly know?

It's essential to question your relationships and to work on ways that will improve your communication and overall happiness with your partner. It's also a good idea, when meeting someone new, to study their intentions and read between the lines. In the first instance, when your hormones are taking over, it's easy to get carried away and forget some of the basic principles of what makes for a great relationship that is going to endure.

You're probably wondering where to start. Are you in a relationship currently? Are you looking for love, but finding it difficult to choose between two or more people? Are you simply not able to meet someone? Well, there are some basic questions you can ask yourself to discover the truth of just how well suited you and your partner are for each other. If you don't have a partner at the moment, you might like to reflect on your previous relationships to improve your chances next time round.

The following quiz is a serious attempt to take an honest look at yourself and see whether or not your relationships are on track. Don't rush through the questionnaire, but think carefully about your practical day-to-day life and whether or not the relationship you are in genuinely fulfils your needs and the other person's needs. There's no point being in a relationship if you're gaining no satisfaction out of it.

Now, if you aren't completely satisfied with the results you get, don't give up! It's an opportunity for you to work at the relationship and to improve things. But you mustn't let your ego get in the road, because that's not going to get you anywhere.

As an Aries, you're fully dedicated to the spirit of passion and emotions. You need a partner who can flow with your temperament and needs. Some might even say you are a very high-maintenance individual. You probably agree. You have certain unique requirements in order to be happy in your romantic life. So here's a checklist for you, Aries, to see if he or she's the right one for you.

Scoring System:

Yes = 1 point

No = 0 points

❓ Does he or she adore and respect you?

❓ Does he or she make you proud?

❓ Does he or she compromise?

❓ Does he or she believe in talking rather than quarrelling or nagging?

❓ Does he or she treat you like a king or queen?

❓ Is he or she there for you all the time?

❓ Is he or she outgoing?

❓ Is he or she independent?

❓ Does he or she possess a sense of adventure?

❓ Does your partner make you the centre of his or her attention?

❓ Does he or she offer you compliments?

❓ Is he or she a sensitive, delicate romantic?

❓ Does he or she give you space sometimes, when it's needed?

❓ Is he or she faithful to you?

❓ Does he or she sexually satisfy you?

❓ Were they born under the signs of Leo, Sagittarius, Aquarius or Gemini?

Have you jotted down your answers honestly? If you're finding it hard to come up with the correct answers, let your intuition help and try not to force them. Of course, there's no point pretending and turning a blind eye to treatment that is less than acceptable, otherwise you're not going to have a realistic appraisal of your prospects with your current love interest. Here are the possible points you can score.

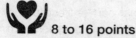

8 to 16 points

A good match. This shows you've obviously done something right, and that the partner you have understands you and is able to reciprocate in just the way you need. But this doesn't mean you should become lazy and not continue working on your relationship. There's always room to improve and make your already excellent relationship even better.

5 to 7 points

Half-hearted prospect. You're going to need to work hard at your relationship, and this will require a close self-examination of just who may be at fault. You know, it takes two to tango, and it's more than likely a combination of both your attitudes is what is dragging down your relationship. Systematically go over each of the above questions and try make a list of where you can improve. I guarantee that your relationship will improve if given some time and sincerity on your part. If, after a genuine effort of working at it, you find things still haven't improved, it may be time for you to rethink your future with this person.

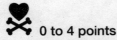

0 to 4 points

On the rocks. I'm sorry to say that this relationship is not founded on a sufficiently strong enough base of mutual respect and understanding. It's likely that the two of you argue a lot, don't see eye to eye or, frankly, have completely different ideas of what sort of lifestyle and emotional needs you each have. The big question here is why are you still with this person?

Again, this requires some honest self-examination to see if there is some inherent insecurity which is causing you to hold onto something that has outgrown its use in your life. Old habits die hard, as they say, and you may also fear letting go of a relationship you have become accustomed to, even though it doesn't fulfil your needs. Self-honesty is the key here. At certain times in life you may need to make some rather big sacrifices to move on to a new phase, which will then hopefully attract the right sort of partner to you.

2012
YEARLY OVERVIEW

IF YOU DON'T DESIGN YOUR OWN
LIFE PLAN, CHANCES ARE YOU'LL FALL
INTO SOMEONE ELSE'S PLAN. AND
GUESS WHAT THEY HAVE PLANNED
FOR YOU? NOT MUCH.

Jim Rohn

⚹ KEY EXPERIENCES ⚹

The most important astrological transits throughout 2012 are those of Saturn, Uranus, Jupiter and Pluto. These planets highlight the importance of recreating yourself, expanding your value system and carefully analysing your relationships.

Transformations continue in your work and self-identity, and once you get this right, everything should flow smoothly. You will feel great about life, relationships and work.

You must learn the art of accepting yourself, and to do this without relying on others to bolster your ego. By increasing your self-awareness and applying yourself to your chosen career, you will gain the respect of others.

ROMANCE AND
✕ FRIENDSHIP ✕

With Venus transiting your zone of friendships as the year commences, you can expect a great time in your romantic and social activities throughout 2012. Furthermore, Neptune, the planet of supreme idealism, is occupying this same zone, meaning that you should expect the best from others and that you will want to receive at least as much as you give from now on. So you need to be careful that you don't put newcomers on a pedestal, thinking they are gods or goddesses, and then find yourself disappointed when you discover that they are, after all, only human.

The big challenge for many Aries-born lovers this year is the continuing trend of Saturn in the zone of marriage and significant partnerships. You will be tested, and you will need to understand that, particularly if you are in an existing relationship, some of the challenges you experience will push you to your limits. Yet on the other hand, persistence, loyalty and accepting the responsibilities of a long-term relationship will bring you some of the greatest joys you have experienced in your life.

ARE YOU SINGLE, ARIES?

*For single Aries this might be a tough year, especially
if you are expecting too much from others. You may
set your sights so high that it will be impossible to meet
the perfect lover. Accept human frailty as part of the
romance equation and you'll be much happier.*

The entry of Uranus into your Sun sign in 2011 was an important development for you, not just in your relationships, but indeed in terms of your evolution as a human being. This progressive planet heralds the beginning of a new approach to relationships and to the way you perceive yourself. You are prepared to try new things in this coming twelve months, and by doing so you will attract some extraordinary circumstances and unusual people who will help accelerate your development personally, professionally and spiritually.

Jupiter, one of your best planets, transits through your zone of communication, and this can only help you in any sort of negotiation and discussion with people closest to you. If you feel that contact with your loved one has stalled, you needn't worry too much about this now. This transit is an excellent pacifier and will bring understanding to any relationship, as long as you are prepared to open your heart and listen a little more to your partner.

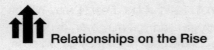 **Relationships on the Rise**

A burst of emotional love-energy is evident in January when the Sun transits your zone of social activities and community involvement. Utilise these energies to make the most of meeting new people.

POPULARITY IN 2012

Venus enters your Sun sign on the 8th of February, and by the 24th, when Venus enjoins your Sun, there is an upswing in your personal popularity and enhanced opportunities for romantic involvements.

For those of you who may be separated from your loved ones by distance, April is an excellent time to reconnect, travel and enjoy cultural exchanges, either together or individually. Venus sets the trend for some sort of international involvement and ties in with romantic escapades.

Educating yourself about the psychological interplays involved in love affairs, romantic involvements and marriage itself will go a long way to help you understand and improve your current and future relationships. There's no shame in making an appointment with a psychologist if you're having problems with your past. Start afresh. A clear mind will assist your perception when you meet new people for whom you think are worth a shot at love.

Venus is retrograde through May and up until June. Relationships could stall, and you'll be left wondering about your personal relationships. People may not be straightforward with you and you may even doubt your own ability to love. Remember these feelings will pass, and don't get too down on yourself about it.

Love affairs may overwhelm you throughout July and August as the Sun transits the creative and loving zone of your horoscope. Once again, in September, Venus will enter this same zone while the Sun simultaneously transits your marital sector. This is most definitely an excellent time to say yes if the big marriage question is popped. For most, however, expect a joyful time with your loved ones. These transits continue up until the end of October.

....

HOT AND STEAMY NOVEMBER

Sex is hot for you in November! Enjoy your physical appetite as much as possible, but don't forget to include the emotional aspects of your relationship to achieve all-round satisfaction in your love life.

....

It's important to appreciate love, and when Venus moves through your ninth zone of luck and karma on the 16th of December, try to express your appreciation by not overlooking gestures of kindness. Your good karma will return paid with interest. Once again, travel with a loved one or close friend is indicated.

❧ WORK AND MONEY ❧

 Harness Your Moneymaking Powers

Making money can be summed up in an equation:

$$m \text{ (\$ money)} = e \text{ (energy)} \times t \text{ (time)} \times l \text{ (love)}$$

If one of the above factors is not present—for example, energy or love—you could still make money, but you won't be ideally fulfilled in the process.

It's absolutely essential to understand the universal laws of attraction and success when speaking about money. It is also necessary to understand that when you love what you do, you infuse your work with the qualities of attention, love and perfection.

With these qualities, you endow your work with a sort of electromagnetic appeal: a power that draws people to your work and causes them to appreciate what you do. This, in turn, generates a desire for people to use your services, buy your products and respect you for the great work you perform. This will without a doubt elevate you to higher and higher positions because you will be regarded as someone who exercises great diligence and skill in your actions.

Uranus is relating to your business profits and it will be in your Sun sign throughout the whole of 2012, demonstrating that you are more likely to be daring about trying something different. This is a new cycle for you and highlights the necessity to think outside the square.

With Jupiter transiting your zone of income you're able to both make and spend money, because this planet's influence is equally as strong on your zone of debt. The moral of the story is: balance your finances. Generosity is a wonderful thing, but if it leaves you short of cash, then it highlights the fact you haven't been judicious enough in managing it.

YEAR OF MOVING AND SHAKING!

Are you feeling stuck in your job, Aries? Have you been treading water and feel as though you're in a professional rut? Well, 2012 is your year to make that move and boldly assert your Aries star power!

Saturn, your primary career planet, is in the dignified star sign of Libra, offering you opportunities to carefully plan your strategy for a brand new career. From April till June you may change direction rather dramatically, and this will be the start of a fantastic new opportunity for you in your profession or chosen career path. Transformation is likely to take place in your profession, but probably not until November, when Saturn moves out of Libra and into the sign of Scorpio. Expect some important progress professionally at this time.

By far the best careers during 2012 are indicated by the sign of Libra, which has to do with the general public, and includes communication, mediation and other sales-related industries. Uranus adds a unique flavour to the combination throughout the coming twelve months by giving you a lift in the search for new or progressive approaches to your professional activities.

March is an excellent time to increase your financial position. Ask your boss for a raise or seek a new job with a more lucrative remuneration package.

June is also an excellent time to sign contracts and to demand the conditions that you want in your work, due to the excellent aspect of Venus on your career planet, Saturn. Venus is the ruler of your income and monetary situation. It's more than likely you will see an increase of cash throughout this period.

In August, Venus once again favourably influences your career sector, while Pluto indicates a deep and profound interest in the line of work you happen to be in. This may take you into a whole new area of study or activity, which will be very exciting.

 Tips for Financial Success

An important tip for tapping into your moneymaking powers is to do things a little differently, especially during February and March, when Venus connects with Uranus and also tenants your second zone of income. Mix things up. Keep others guessing, and don't share your ideas and intellectual property too quickly. Keep a tight rein on your thoughts as well as your money.

Important moneymaking periods include the Sun's transit through your property zone after the 21st of June. Capitalise on real estate negotiations, sell property and increase your investment power through fixed assets such as land and housing. Interior design or decoration is a source of creative and financial satisfaction.

You must also take time to speculate or gamble wisely during the Sun's transit in your zone of speculation after the 22nd of July. Once again, don't be crazy with how you spend your money, and if necessary, get some advice on how you can best diversify your investment portfolio to secure your financial future.

The secret to making money is sometimes not spending it, and this is evident. Cut back your expenses, don't be too generous—neither with yourself or others—and will see your bank balance growing.

ECLIPSE HIGHLIGHT

The solar eclipse on the 14th of November is significant for shared resources and money you have with others. Pool your resources with someone who has more knowledge than you and is able to help direct your attention to the appropriate ways of earning money.

Time is as significant as money, and when you run around trying to save a dollar here or a dollar there, that time could cost a lot more. Work carefully on your diary, plan effectively, and by using your time more efficiently, you will start to make more money.

Career Moves and Promotions

Because the Sun dominates your horoscope throughout January, it's imperative to ask for a promotion or pay rise early in the year. Employers will favour you because at this time the Sun brings out your best character, leadership abilities and charm. Do this before the 20th of January.

In March, when Venus comes in to contact with Jupiter in your financial sector (around the 14th), excellent planetary conditions step up your financial earnings a notch or two. There is a risk that seeing more cash in your pocket could give you a false sense of security, so your spending could be big. Save your money.

NEGOTIATION HOT SPOT

Contracts are positive after the 21st of May, especially around the 6th of June, when the Sun and Venus influence your contracts. A win-win situation will occur at this time and even the fine print may surprise you with unexpected benefits.

Speculate on opportunities after the 22nd of July. With the Sun moving in your fifth zone of creativity up until the 23rd of August, you'll be noticed for your excellent craftsmanship, skill in action and the ability to negotiate with others.

Make those appropriate workplace changes throughout August, especially after the 23rd, when you could feel bored and need a breath of fresh air as far as work and co-workers are concerned. It could be time to move on if you are feeling stale.

Finally, the Sun returns to the uppermost part of your horoscope after the 21st of December, just before Christmas Day. Many Aries-born individuals will find the latter part of the year promising for professional prospects. Harness these energies and use them to approach your employer with whatever request you feel is fair.

When to Avoid Office Politics

Office politics seem to be part and parcel of work these days, so it's good to know when antagonistic, stressful days are going to ruffle your feathers.

Mercury and Mars create havoc in communication between the 14th and 28th January. You'll be edgy, and it'll be best to keep your mouth closed so that what you say isn't misinterpreted by co-workers.

Underhanded tactics employed by others need to be carefully monitored after the 15th of March. Pluto creates problems with those who may be interested in wresting power from you. These influences are in place until the 8th of May.

Misunderstandings are likely due to Mercury, between the 6th and the 10th of May, and then between the 26th and the 31st, so avoid important meetings when your words could be twisted.

June the 12th till the 21st is another critical period when it's best to write rather than speak. Others may not hear what you have to say, at least in the way you intended it, and this can cause problems.

Disputes are likely in the third week of July due to the action of Mars. Reduce your stress levels with some exercise or outdoor activity.

You'll need to get to the bottom of things in the last weeks of September, particularly between the 21st and the 25th. You mustn't believe everything you hear. Research things for yourself so that you will be satisfied with your findings.

You could be confused about your work and issues of loyalty between the 30th of October and the 7th of November. At this time you will need to go back over some old issues to regain some clarity.

Another bout of confusion and possible misunderstandings with employees or clients is likely around the 11th of December. Make sure your communication encompasses everything you intend it to.

HEALTH, BEAUTY AND
❧ LIFESTYLE ❧

 Venus Calendar for Beauty

Venus, Goddess of Beauty and Love, also works as your relationship planet, Aries. During 2012, its movement through the zodiac indicates when you are likely to be your most magnetic and persuasive, especially if you are trying to attract others.

After the 8th of February, when Venus enters your Sun sign, and up to and including the 24th, you will feel more alive and your skin will glow with a particular beauty. This is one of the most excellent periods of the year to socialise, go online and meet new people, and even accept a blind date. There's every likelihood of your turning on the charm and attracting a new suitor.

You should also have regular beauty therapy, hair styling, manicuring and massages, especially in the early part of the year, to set the trend for the next few months. By feeling good you will look good as well.

You may not know why, but after the 22nd of November your sexual magnetism is very powerful, and this has to do with Venus transiting through your eighth zone of sexuality and hidden powers. You must never abuse this privilege, but should certainly use it to your advantage, if you can, to gain the upper hand over competitors in the romance department.

Finally, Venus is lucky for you from the 16th up until the 30th of December, because it enhances such things as your good fortune, travels, higher knowledge, physical attractiveness and willpower. All of these dates are excellent omens, and you can expect the year to be full of vibrant new opportunities to express your beauty and enjoy the benefits of it.

<hr />

BEAUTY CYCLES

Other times of the year when Venus and the Sun activate your inner beauty and attractiveness include the period around the 2nd of June, the 7th of July, the 7th of September and between the 11th and the 28th of October. This last period is extraordinarily powerful for offering long-term relationships, and a deep sense of love and satisfaction, because of the favourable vibrations of this loving planet.

<hr />

 Showing off Your Aries Traits

Each zodiac sign has its own unique power based on the elements and planets that rule it. Unfortunately, most people don't know how to tap into this power and bring out their greatest potential to achieve success in life.

Mars is your ruling planet and, as such, it indicates the great power and fighting spirit that you possess. Unfortunately, sometimes you are unable to harness its energy in the proper manner, causing you to lose this energy, which can otherwise be used to achieve your goals much quicker.

Slowing your pace is essential if you are going to achieve your destiny happily and gain the support of everyone around you. Irritability, aggression and other temperamental outbursts will not be received well by those who you'd like to support you. So remember, staying calm is the way to bring out the best Aries flavours within you.

MONTHS OF POWER

When your ruling planet, Mars, is in strength throughout 2012, you can make the best of your personal characteristics to achieve success, attract good people and enjoy your life to the max. The important Mars cycles include the months of July and August, and late November and December.

During the transits of Mars you will feel at your peak, and others will notice your energy and magnetism more than they would at other times of the year.

You have the opportunity to make a big impact on the world during August, but be careful not to lose heart if your enthusiasm is not initially met with optimism. The combination of Mars and Saturn at this time will indicate a slow but steady process, as long as you don't throw in the towel and quit.

By far the best period to express yourself and your strong personality is in November and December, when your professional life will be served well by your ruling planet. Enjoy all the benefits that come to you at this time.

Best Ways to Celebrate

When you celebrate your birthday, anniversary and other important events, it's important for friends and loved ones to understand that the Aries temperament is not at all partial to boring or lifeless situations.

Bright, bold and exciting activities must be part of the situation to capture your imagination and attention. You also like to be a little different, as shown by Aquarius being in your zone of social activities. Anything that sets you apart from others and stimulates your friends is an ideal way for you to enjoy life.

Car races, sporting events and other loud and active environments are perfect parties for the Aries individual. It's also best to choose people who are communicative, creative and fun loving. If you're invited somewhere too relaxed, you're likely to fall asleep or depart early. You just will not waste your time hanging around a bunch of deadbeats or couch potatoes.

In 2012, some of the best periods to celebrate and enjoy life include March and early April. During this cycle, Venus and Jupiter, the two beneficial planets, combine in your zone of money, so it could be that you will have reason to celebrate by way of some increase, a pay rise or even a lucky windfall.

Family festivities are on the cards during the transit of Venus in late August, and throughout September and October. You will enjoy partying with family members and friends within the comfort of your own home. Romantic celebrations are also indicated at this time, as well as a huge upliftment in your marital prospects. An engagement and marriage around November—yours or that of someone you know—is likely.

KARMA, SPIRITUALITY AND EMOTIONAL ✕ BALANCE ✕

Your primary spiritual and karmic planets are Jupiter, the Sun and Neptune. They indicate the best possible ways for you to find peace and harmony in 2012.

Neptune is a planet of idealism and is located at the tail end of your social zone until the latter part of February. Try to connect with friends on a deeper level, give them more time and try to understand where they are coming from. Being short of time is a poor excuse for not giving the appropriate attention to the ones who love you most.

SPIRITUAL HIGHLIGHT

Once Neptune moves into your twelfth zone of spirituality and secrets, you'll have ample time to dedicate to yourself and your inner needs. This is also highlighted by the Sun, which will be in conjunction with Neptune at this time. Up until April it's okay to remain alone. The Sun will then return to Aries, bringing with it an increased level of energy and interest in the world.

The most prominent spiritual planet for you is Jupiter, and throughout the period of January until June you will be focused on material affairs, money and issues of security. However, you mustn't get lost in this maze of worldly concerns. Spare some time to find yourself, get acquainted with peace and quiet, and plug into the creative subconscious that you may have overlooked for some time.

It's imperative for you to keep your feet planted firmly on the ground as Jupiter transits the practical sign of Taurus. You need to do things in which you can see tangible results. And you must do this before Jupiter transits to the air sign, Gemini, which will herald a new phase to do with the beginnings of ideas and plans for the future.

The Sun is exceptionally well placed from the 16th of July up until the 30th. Creative activities, sporting functions and other ways of releasing tension and decompressing your emotional difficulties are well advised. Competitive activities will bring you a great deal of success.

Paying attention to your health throughout August and September will further help you find peace and clarity. Try to get involved in some sort of sport that doesn't make you prone to injury. Light, brisk, but non-stressful forms of exercise are best for you at this time.

The Sun enters the highly spiritual sign of Sagittarius in your zone of higher learning, travels and spirituality on the 16th of November. This is a period where study, travel, and higher forms of knowledge and philosophy may be ways to unwind, gaining a deeper understanding of yourself and life.

2012
MONTHLY & DAILY PREDICTIONS

BLESSED IS HE WHO EXPECTS
NOTHING, FOR HE SHALL NEVER BE
DISAPPOINTED.

Anonymous

❧ JANUARY ❧

 Monthly Highlight

Mercury and Mars cause friction in the first week of January, but channel this energy and you'll achieve great things at work. Mars moves retrograde on the 24th, while Mercury and Saturn slow things up, causing frustrations. Hang in there because Mercury increases your profits after the 28th.

1 You may feel that a new responsibility or work achievement may clash with personal needs. Don't worry—the two will converge in their own good time.

2 Today you may not be open in your dealings with others, so try to avoid super egos. You may suddenly act passively or aggressively. Even so, someone will try to bait you.

3 To move forward today you'll have to tap into your inner resources. Don't become obsessive about money—this may separate you from your intimate relationships.

4 Today you could feel hurt and unappreciated. However, this may bring you to an awareness of your own shortfalls so you can then advance and rise above a sense of neediness.

5 Take time out to listen to conventional wisdom today, because your 'listening' ears may not be open. You could be reckless and fiery. Practical guidance will help you channel into creative pursuits.

6 Mould your surroundings and make use of plants, fragrances, candles and other artefacts to simulate faraway places. Tranquillity will come from your imagination. Communicate ideas.

7 Today you may be prone to philosophical fanaticism, rejecting normal friendships based on people's belief systems and values. Compromise or you may get others offside.

8 You may invite trouble today in your family circles by not agreeing with a good idea. You'll feel bored with tradition, so do your own thing and avoid the hassle.

9 Your mouth may be on autopilot...don't finish other people's sentences for them! Attend to home issues because they affect your psychological health today.

10 You can channel your Martian moods and energy to provide useful suggestions to loved ones. Do this subtly and you will gain some benefits in a roundabout way.

11 A troublesome issue is repeating in your mind over and over, like a scratched record. Today's lesson is to move your mind into a thought-free state. Remain peaceful!

12 Don't deny spontaneity in your personality today. You might be absorbed in doing the job right and thereby forget the greater power of who you *are*. Be aware.

13 Recent confusion in your work gives way to an enlightened view of a current association that's been skewed as a result of your rose-coloured glasses.

14 You can either get caught up in the same old patterns with co-workers, or try a different approach today. A bit of reverse psychology will go a long way.

15 The Moon is influenced by Saturn today, and the forces shaping your romantic destiny could seem dull. Luckily, your grievance and doubt over a relationship is short lived.

16 You're feeling confident, even though Mercury could be tempting you to feel down about some of your less-than-desirable character traits. Remain positive!

17 You think you've resolved a buried issue with someone who tampered with your emotions. Retrace your mental steps to discover why a relationship ended the way it did.

18 Emotional responsibility is weighing heavily upon you. This next 24 hours will see a need to resolve some issues from older members of your family or someone at work.

19 Someone's not showing you the affection you deserve just now. You've thrown enough hints, but for some reason they're flying over that person's head. Don't compare them with others.

20 Your desire for travel is at a peak today. Your generous and compassionate attitude will repay you tenfold and bring emotional satisfaction. Share a holiday, or at least a day off, with a friend.

21 Power-tripping is part of the game some co-workers want to play. Employ some new tactics to deal with people who are ruthless—put them in their place!

22 A friend needs your guidance in the art of war. Divided loyalties represent a problem for you because the third party they're warring with is also a friend of yours...

23 Sometimes you have to boil down the sap to get to the syrup. Look a little more deeply and see the true worth of a special person you may have met recently.

24 Don't overdo your perfume, colour or fashion statement today. Subtlety is a delicate art when applied to those people you wish to impress. Use your natural charm.

25 There are prospects for an exciting and nicely challenging day today, but only if you make an effort to get up and out of your own way. Don't disconnect from friends.

26 Don't get carried away with bits and pieces that have no relationship to the bigger picture. Delegate the small stuff so your single focus is on the bigger picture! Avoid confusing issues.

27 If you're home or job hunting, today is the day when you could find success in the form of an offer or referral. Settle for no less than what you believe is fair! Do research online.

28 Take advantage of the progressive influences coming your way today. Unhappy family situations reach a turning point and you're the meat in the sandwich!

29 Your social life is on an upward climb today, with invitations reaching you in the most unusual of ways! Wear that favourite shade of maroon for extra support!

30 Financial satisfaction requires hard work now. A financial move is scary, but you will be so relieved with the outcome—as long as you don't doubt yourself in the process.

31 An excellent work opportunity is around the corner. Investigate what's on offer and make some enquiries by being proactive. A hint from a friend will inspire you.

⊱ FEBRUARY ⊰

Monthly Highlight

Focus on spiritual affairs this month by staying away from others. Don't let your mind become confused after the 14th. Mercury and Neptune make you forget things and you're unclear in communication. By the 28th you'll feel much better about yourself and a promotion is possible.

1 The climate is fine for financial strategies to take pride of place in your agenda. Look carefully at who is going to be involved in the moneymaking process. There'll be some support from a close friend, so snap it up!

2 Try not to be sidetracked by what everyone else is doing today. Focus on what you have to create to ensure all your senses are satisfied. Eat before you start!

3 Let everyday worries pass you by, and welcome the amazing fun and laughter that could be offered to you from unexpected sources today. It's time to take up an energetic new hobby.

4   If a promise is broken, you can bet you haven't trusted your instincts in the first place, or you could've applied too much pressure. Take time out to reassess.

5   Someone who's been a large part of your life could offer you something you've been longing for. It'll come as a complete surprise, possibly through someone within your family.

6   Mention what you are happy with before you tackle what you're not! The pressure of conducting an event will take its toll, but try to take it in your stride.

7   Today may involve wiping away someone's tears, and perhaps you were the cause. You've forgotten something important or left things wide open for doubt. The black cloud will lift quickly.

8   There is a lot of activity sorting out some romantic matters and revamping your approach to love. This could mean harvesting more emotional responses from your partner.

9   You'll struggle with an unexpected decision concerning a workplace feud or job opportunity. Consider and accept that you and someone else need not consult each other on the matter.

10 As far as your work direction is concerned, it's a big step for you to take at this stage. But when you do the maths and weigh up the pros and cons, the only way to move is forward.

11 If you prefer to do things the way you have found to be efficient, talk to your boss or partner to see if your needs can be accommodated without affecting the job. A novel approach is necessary.

12 Now that things are totally clear, it won't take much to get things up and running with everyone onside. You'll have to compromise to have the whole world smiling.

13 It's a case of getting what you are given and liking it today! You'll have to contend with disappointment, but be tactful with the other person…things may just go your way.

14 Before you listen to others, have a think about what you're wanting from the situation. A succinct phone conversation or e-mail with someone at a distance should clear the air.

15 Recently, you were certain that you didn't want to make a move. Today you will be totally brave and start making plans for a new and exciting change in your life.

16 You may want to look over travel brochures a little more carefully before signing on the dotted line, and listen carefully to your heart. Ask yourself if this is really what you want?

17 If you feel duped by someone who hasn't paid you what you're worth, this might be the day to speak your mind. Fair is fair. Ask for what you deserve!

18 Expect a sudden turn of events at work. Unforeseen actions cause tension and irrational decision making on your part. Don't act impulsively until you have all the information.

19 It's time to turn over a new leaf. The new Moon means you have to say no. Someone insists on disrupting your daily timetable and you need to put your foot down. Set some limits!

20 Your social life is on the upswing today. It won't be long before you get some positive news. Start making plans and remain positive that your ambition for social acceptance will work.

21 According to some reliable people, you're not to blame, so you shouldn't be beating yourself up about it! A fresh perspective is what is needed and will tell you their information is correct.

22 Before you go making it your business to take care of everyone around you, ensure you don't jeopardise your immediate responsibilities or your own personal needs.

23 Share a brilliant new idea in a workplace meeting. Don't be shy. You want things to work out as you've envisioned, so do your best to say what you feel creatively.

24 Intuitively, you will come to a decision about some family friction. It's imperative that there's no dredging up of old stories. Leave them well and truly in the past.

25 An excellent day to make changes to your routine and the way you look. Find out what's necessary for your long-range goals because these plans are going to be your new life foundations.

26 Did you know that when the going gets rough, the tough stick around to see what they can reap out of the situation? Some much-needed romance is shown to you later in the day.

27 It'll be pointless trying to make out you know what is going on when those who love you know you have little idea! Embrace the new and be gentle on yourself. Don't over-embellish a story.

28 Prepare yourself for a day when everything could become confusing. You only have limited energy and time to put into people and their problems. Give a thought to delegation.

29 Your skills in communicating a problem to someone will be the key to making peace, not war. Don't complicate your words; keep things simple and speak from the heart.

❊ MARCH ❊

🏋 *Monthly Highlight*

Educational matters feature strongly throughout March. You'll learn new things and apply yourself to a new course of study. It's best to do this before the 12th. Power issues affect you after the 15th, so be careful not to be too secretive, as friends may mistrust you.

1 A push in the right direction from someone can turn your life around today, helping you get out to explore the world and see what else is on offer in your life. Break out of your routine and take some new steps.

2 Take advantage of a shoulder to cry on, even if that isn't easy for you. A friend will listen without judgement and help clear the air on some past concerns.

3 A surprise visit from someone who you've wanted to talk to should brighten your day, but it could cause problems with family members who have alternative plans. Discuss the get-together with others first.

4 Whatever you do, don't disregard the feelings of your partner when it comes to your choice of friends. That could be the cause of suspicion, which you need to alleviate.

5 Your most intimate life has overcome some hurdles. Once the difficult patches are over, things will be back to normal and far better than you could have imagined.

6 There is much to be said for people who grab the bull by the horns to experience life and romantic potentials. Forget about being the happy tortoise today. Take what is on offer.

7 Your thoughts are being influenced by others with little concept of how the whole thing should look. Think for yourself if you want to make an impression, and don't argue the point.

8 Keep your wits about you when faced with a situation that could make you feel overwhelmed. Don't worry—there'll be support to help you in the race today.

9 Count to ten or breathe deeply before you open your mouth, especially if a particular individual is of nuisance value. Don't share everything with them just now.

10 You could have a huge desire to break down barriers between yourself and others who have been distant recently, although initially it may just take an apology on your part.

11 Cutting off your nose to spite your face is something you'll need to watch today. The best way to approach things would be to listen, especially to your lover.

12 Your joy in serving someone until you can't serve them any more could be in need of attention today. Give some quality time towards expressing some love.

13 Confidence and magnetism will allow you to make full use of your power. However, with numerous activities on your agenda, be less self-centred and a little more compassionate.

14 Seek out people with whom you wouldn't normally spend time, in the hope of learning more to get a project up and running. They will provide the break you're looking for.

15 Ready to get your teeth into a new area of study or a hobby that could eventually bring rewards you had no idea were even a possibility? It's time now, but still quite a challenge!

16 An ignorant and cowardly act by someone leaves you high and dry, but also makes you much stronger. Use this to gain greater understanding and help others in similar situations.

17 An improvement in your work skills will make your employer pay attention. Set the record straight and show them that you are capable in your chosen profession.

18 If you see a co-worker struggling with something you've recently delegated, be patient and explain it all once again. Then wait for a job well done!

19 You can expect to make an impressive comeback with your peers in a new social environment. This is guaranteed to kick-start your game, so the lethargic spell seems to be over.

20 You might miss the meaning behind what a person is actually trying to say today! Don't stand for the mish-mash dialogue. Romance takes a nice turn, however.

21 Avoid confusion when offering money to friends; it is best to get a commitment from them on its repayment. You don't want to mix finances with friendship because this could cause a breakdown in relations.

22 It's an ideal day to strut your stuff and show that you have leadership potential. The benefits could be quite tangible. Some financial surprises are also in store.

23 You'll have trouble deciding what is of value and what is not. You need to avoid the opinions of others if you are going to make a rational decision about these key issues in your life. Spend time alone to do it.

24 You are sentimental today, but don't let this get in the way of a proper decision. You're wearing your heart on your sleeve and not seeing another person in the correct light. Be a little ruthless in your judgement.

25 There are several opportunities to increase your bank balance and possibly commence something new in your career. You mustn't be afraid. If you don't have enough confidence, then develop it.

26 You're well directed in your energies today, but what you say may be misconstrued. Be softer in your approach, even if you think you are already being considerate of the other person's point of view.

27 You are out of step with some of the people in your environment today. It's best to remain silent because your attitude or perspective may not be appreciated. Silence is golden.

28 Your communication centres on things from the past. However, don't get bogged down in the negative aspects of this. Gloss over arrogant comments or critical statements aimed at you.

29 A short journey is fruitful today. Step out of your normal environment to explore other avenues that will fulfil you and give you a greater sense of the world at large.

30 Your thinking is big, so don't let anyone else try to cut you down to their size. Tall poppy syndrome seems to be in play today. Believe in your dreams, and go for it.

31 You are much quieter than normal and will want to spend time at home, but this should not come from feeling dejected or angry at others. Resolve some issues before nightfall.

✢ APRIL ✢

Monthly Highlight

Getting down to the details of your work is essential. You must not get into debt. You could be impulsive after the 14th. Due to the Sun and Uranus, conflicts arise in your personal affairs. Be clear about your intentions and plan your actions in consultation first.

1 Making new friends, exploring new avenues of communication and even developing your existing romantic affiliations are all on the cards right now.

2 A little bit too much push in your nature can result in some physical injury if you're not careful. You have an immense drive to get things done. Slow down.

3 There's a breakthrough in the continuing saga of responsibility versus freedom…Your family and loved ones support your choices and chosen path, after all.

4   You've been wanting to spend more time alone, but pressing social and family demands won't allow that to happen. You'll have to move your own needs to the end of the list today.

5   Part of you wants to sever ties with someone, but you're aware of the poor timing. Best to forget any grievances you might have, then make a move if you must.

6   You've still got some concerns over money, or rather, the lack thereof. There could be a disagreement with your significant other over the spending of money.

7   Your value system has changed in the last couple of years. The glamorous, glitzy partying of the past doesn't appeal to you as much as the quiet life.

8   If you are in a committed relationship, you may not receive the affectionate response you need today, in spite of your attempts to show your love to another.

9   You'll be restless and probably not very patient with any type of routine. Serious people will irritate you, so keep away from them today!

10 The extravagance and wild reactions of someone could confuse and upset you today. Your heightened sensitivity may not be conducive to the company of high-energy people.

11 You could become very strong and unaffected when dealing with the weaknesses and shortcomings of others today. You shouldn't allow their fears or envy to harm you.

12 You could get involved in a questionable romance during this period, managing to fall in love with an illusion rather than a real person. Be careful.

13 Your way of thinking can be affected by tension or radical changes in your immediate surroundings. Free yourself from taboos or other unconscious beliefs.

14 Your ideas won't be totally understood or accepted by people around you, and they could provoke disagreements and changes in the way you communicate.

15 Your relationships with people in authority will be very promising just now because you are more than willing to fulfil what they ask of you.

16 This is a very favourable time for marriage, relationship possibilities and a very warm, fulfilling home life, giving you the security and stability you seek.

17 You will be more compassionate, caring, sympathetic and supportive of the people around you, and they will respond the same way for the good of all.

18 You may take new risks in things you wouldn't have attempted otherwise. Things naturally seem to gravitate to you and turn out to be very beneficial today.

19 Today you will find that your need to succeed and accomplish something is quite overwhelming, for both yourself and people around you. You may be a little possessive.

20 Business matters seem to be under a fortunate star just now. You can expect to make some real progress materially, socially and intellectually.

21 It's amazing how much better you'll feel when gripes are out in the open, particularly with those you felt didn't pull their weight in a joint activity.

22 It's almost certain you'll make it your business to take on board a position that will up the ante on your weekly income and add prestige to your daily life.

23 You'll be tempted to dive into a business deal or residential offer that could put you behind the eight-ball financially if you don't read the small print.

24 After all this time you still find the same feelings come up in association with a certain situation. It's time you reassessed where you're going with this.

25 Everything is spinning around in your head—you are letting yourself be run by other people's problems and fears. Time to get into a better shape mentally.

26 With a need for power, you may stoop to sneaky or underhanded methods to get what you want. Learn to recognise your own and others' limits and tolerance levels.

27 There may be a real conflict in professional matters or domestic affairs and you can easily feel isolated, unloved and lonely. You will need support from others.

28 You may become reclusive, shunning contacts with others for a while…Your new values will be an orderly existence, along with neatness and organisation.

29 You'll find yourself demanding a lot from others and being bossy. There will be extravagance in money matters, where you can easily go overboard with luxuries.

30 You won't be satisfied until you have the biggest and best of anything in your path today. Everything will be done in a big way and, as a result, you may be spreading yourself too thinly.

✕ MAY ✕

Monthly Highlight

Both the new Moon and the full Moon affect your finances, therefore your attention will be focused on these matters. You could be reactive due to the presence of the Moon and Mars, so don't respond to anything until you have a clear picture based upon facts and figures. Mercury causes you to seek out fun after the 17th.

---

1 You need to trust your gut instincts when it comes to dealing with issues of family and home. Strong karmic planets influence your relationships with children and youngsters.

---

2 A friend may be having a problem similar to one you've just been through. You may be able to help, but remember that you are different people.

---

3 Today would be an excellent time to begin a regular exercise regime together with someone else—such as walking or running—for fitness and for pleasure.

---

4 This could be a harmonious time for your love life. Showing your genuine affection will bring joy back to you many times over.

5 Romantic surprises may come your way with an impulsive or sudden change of heart about a venue or an event you had planned.

6 There may be minor friction in your love life just now, so look at how you may have been behaving lately and what has been said.

7 Checking that you have everything before leaving on a journey, even if just to work, is always a good thing. No purse or wallet? Check again.

8 A trip or journey could spark new insights and make you feel rather content. Surprising solutions to problems will come out of the blue.

9 You may need to get more information from a reliable source before you can make a decision that has far-reaching effects for you.

10 You have a positive mental attitude that will get you through your day, but you also need the correct information for a project.

11 Festive events and social gatherings are favoured, so put work or serious matters on the backburner for a while, and let romance take the front seat.

12 You may have someone around you who thinks they are just that little bit better than you are. Is it really worth worrying about what they think?

13 A quiet weekend away or a special dinner might be just the thing to put a bit of pep back into your love life. Pick up the phone!

14 You may be asked to comfort a friend who is having problems in their relationship. They really just want you to listen, not talk.

15 'If in doubt, leave it out', seems to be the motto for you today. Issues could be clouded, and you need to be sure what it is you want.

16 Make sure your diet is supporting your hectic lifestyle. Good food and exercise will give you the energy you need for the job at hand.

17 Some younger people may just have the answers you've been seeking about a certain situation. Listen and take their opinions on board.

18 Your intuition usually stands you in good stead and today is no exception. Your gut feeling should come before the opinion of others.

19 You may feel your health is not up to par. Check it out thoroughly and do your own research. You know your own body best.

20 You could be having financial issues, but are they really all your fault? Think back on advice given and by whom. Trust your own instincts.

21 A break with routine will lift your spirits and give you a new lease on life. Staying in a five-star hotel may be just the thing.

22 Your level of vitality may need a boost so you can achieve the 101 things you need to do. Look at what you eat each day.

23 You may find things at home not quite to your liking at the moment, but there's no need to stay in all the time and not go out, is there?

24 You may feel as though you're being ignored by the people closest to you, but you probably haven't noticed that they've got issues, too.

25 You may have to trust your intuition about not wanting to go to a certain place with someone or spend two hours hating where you are.

26 There could be something unexpected, unusual or surprising occurring in your love life to bring you an exciting and romantic time ahead.

27 Harmony reigns in your relationship now and, while you are both more interested in the other's happiness, this will continue.

28 Keep control of your anger and don't let irritation flare up when speaking to your boss. Understanding and communication will conquer all—you just need to look a bit deeper for answers.

29 You may have a last-minute job that needs completing and the only way to get it done is to settle down and attack it bit by bit.

30 Currents of warmth and magnetic attraction are flowing in your realm of romance. It is a great time to respond passionately.

31 Beware of taking offence at actions or remarks that really are not intended to hurt you, because this can cause you unnecessary heartache.

⊱ JUNE ⊰

Monthly Highlight

You won't go very far if you don't communicate your feelings. The Moon and Saturn indicate a cooling off period and, particularly on the 1st, 27th and 28th, you need to share your feelings openly. The full Moon on the 30th reflects a deepening in your understanding of your sexual needs.

---

1 Although romance brings a glow to your world, sometimes it is necessary to pull back and have a few days of good quality solitude.

---

2 Something particularly personal and intimate about a special someone could give you cause for hesitation, but trust your gut feelings.

---

3 Hurt feelings can surface and cause a lot of grief in a relationship. But with love, understanding and communication, it will work out.

---

4 Your high estimation of someone is being questioned. Don't let your integrity be brought into question, and go with your intuition.

---

5   You may have to do a little bit of bending and stretching of your calendar to get everything done. Do it, but don't overdo it.

6   Your desire for success could lead you down paths you previously never thought to go. Don't be afraid of success, because it is due to you.

7   It may be time to stop hiding your talents and let the world know what you're capable of. This is an opportunistic time for you.

8   Someone in your social circle may coerce you into going to a play or film that doesn't interest you. A surprise could be in store.

9   Fear and insecurity can be a barrier to love and intimacy, and it would be wise to take a look at yourself rather than blame others.

10   You have the chance to prove others wrong when they say that you're self-absorbed and possibly even selfish. Let them eat their words.

11   There may be someone you consider a close friend who is not working in your best interests. Keep your eyes open for this person.

12 Reservations about a relationship may be causing a few hiccups in your romantic life just now, but watch out for any hidden rivalry.

13 Seen some photos of yourself that you feel are less than flattering? It is possible they were taken for just that reason, you know.

14 You have the drive to do the job and just need to keep focused. Certain financial aspects of your business life may be worrying you.

15 Consider the similarities and differences in another other person's attitude to finances. They may not think and feel the same way you do.

16 You could be in two minds about a purchase that is going to cost much more than you'd originally bargained on. If in doubt, leave it out.

17 You could take some time out to revitalise your romance in a beautiful setting. It doesn't need to be expensive, just romantic.

18 You may be trying to complete a project on time, but are being pulled in all directions by unknown forces conspiring against you.

19 You should keep your wits about you when dealing with new people in your workplace or social circle. They may not be what they seem.

20 You may have stronger feelings of family and nurturing emerging. There could be an older person who needs your help just now.

21 It might not be wise to blurt out your true feelings about someone at the moment. Tread carefully and pick your time to let them know.

22 The feeling of love will give your creativity a boost, and it may be the ideal time to create something beautiful and long-lasting together.

23 Enjoying another person's presence is one of the joys of your romance today. A simple walk along the beach will revitalise intimacy with your partner.

24 You may have the urge to spend a little more than you should at the moment, so go and look through your wardrobe before shopping.

25 Competitiveness is always thrilling, and perhaps you can share that thrill in a romantic way with someone who means a lot to you.

26 Someone may unexpectedly ask you for help. Give it generously and gladly and good fortune will come back to you by the bucket load.

27 Looking closely at someone's flaws is not conducive to a wonderful and loving romance. To err is human and this time it might be you who is at fault.

28 A spirit of decisiveness, action and positive forces infuses your romantic world, so share your dreams and plans with someone special.

29 Others may be trying to control issues directly affecting you, but keep your wits about you, and make your point of view quite clear.

30 You may have to look a little deeper inside yourself to give your partner what they need. Trust your heart and soul.

⚼ JULY ⚼

Monthly Highlight

The month commences with a professional flavour due to the full Moon of the 3rd in your career zone. There is a shift to affairs of the heart around the 19th, with the new Moon in your zone of love affairs. Love is also in the air around the 15th and 16th. Let your hair down and enjoy this energy.

---

1 Be aware of what's happening in the world outside of your own. Someone could give you a tip or information on a moneymaking venture.

---

2 Don't be surprised to receive a call that puts you on the spot. It's always okay to say no and you don't need to explain, either.

---

3 A little flexibility in your attitude could reap great rewards. Not everyone thinks and moves at the speed you do.

---

4 Your career, reputation and role in the community are important to you just now, so make sure no one is spouting bad press about you.

5   Keeping a relationship interesting is a daily challenge and one that many people ignore. A surprise now and again will do the trick.

6   You may have a certain restlessness about you today, but by all means, catch up with friends in a well-known bar or restaurant.

7   There's no use crying over spilt milk or, in your case, lost money. Learn from your errors. Read the fine print next time, please.

8   You may need to take some time out to deal with romantic issues. Keep your feelings away from prying eyes and keep your loved one at a distance until you work it out.

9   Don't speak before thinking and then have to try to explain what you really meant. This will put you on the back foot in romance.

10   Your originality is the key to being understood and appreciated. Be patient with what others have to say. Sit quietly and listen.

11   You need to keep your sense of humour when dealing with difficult people in your workplace, because they can make life very unpleasant.

12 Looking good is great for the ego, but spending more than you should is just as bad for the bank account. Think before you shop.

13 You may be presented with an opportunity that seems too good to be true. Make sure you know the person before accepting them at face value.

14 Someone may choose to discuss personal matters today that you find uncomfortable. Don't be afraid to voice your opinion, even if it hurts.

15 The impression others have of you may not be as accurate as they think. Use your communication skills to get your point across.

16 You may need to do some further negotiating to extract yourself from an uncomfortable situation in which you've found yourself.

17 You may not feel appreciated today, and simply want some space to work out where your relationship is going with someone.

18 There could be a person from your past who reappears in another guise. It's likely they've had a makeover of some sort recently.

19 The new Moon today reminds you that a fresh romance can sometimes leave old friends out in the cold. Remember those who previously stood by you.

20 Expecting another person to exactly fit your ideal picture is being a little too hopeful. Focus on the positive, not the negative.

21 You may meet someone with whom you share a karmic past. Be open to what they have to offer and you could be pleasantly surprised.

22 You must keep an eye on any direct debits from your bank accounts because mistakes do happen. An empty account is not an option!

23 You can't be responsible for what everybody else does in the workplace. Each person needs to take responsibility for themselves.

24 A relationship needs nurturing if it is to grow and blossom, and it is a trap to fall into too much complacency and boredom. Creatively keep your romance alive.

25 You need a mental reboot, so to speak. Clear your memory banks and preconceptions before meetings or other social engagements, and this way your ideas will be more understandable.

26 You have become so wrapped up in someone that you miss what is going on in the rest of the world. Have your friends disappeared?

27 A sense of belonging with another person is a supreme experience, but not one to be taken lightly. Care and attention is needed today.

28 Your partner may not understand what you are going on about, so the motto today is: 'say what you mean, and mean what you say'.

29 You may have to look a little deeper inside yourself to give your partner what they need from you. Trust your heart and soul.

30 You may feel that things are moving too slowly at work, but there could be a perfectly good reason for this—one that is not apparent to everyone just now.

31 You could be getting very tired swimming against the current in your workplace. Things will turn around and your viewpoint will be appreciated shortly.

⊰ AUGUST ⊱

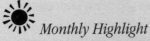

Monthly Highlight

This is a month of friendships, when you connect with existing friends and make new ones. This is highlighted between the 2nd and the 12th. Between the 18th and the 21st, watch your health and don't overdo things. Disputes are likely with a lover after the 21st. Step aside rather than confronting them.

1 Any feelings of hurt should be expressed, yes, but do it in a loving and calm way. Attack is never the best approach.

2 Are there places you'd like to go but feel wouldn't be well received in your relationship? Breathe deeply and go for it.

3 Romance is not only for the young, nor is it wasted on the old, but it is certainly something that needs a daily workout of love.

4 Meditative practices offer you an opportunity to recharge your worn-out batteries. Step aside from people who are giving you a hard time. Pay attention to where you leave valuables.

5 Sometimes listening is all that is needed in a close relationship, and if you can do this, you'll have most of your problems solved.

6 Looking back over your shoulder is not the ideal way to move forward, and can put extra strain on a new and wonderful romance.

7 You will want to be outlandish today in the way you present yourself to others. While this will be fun, bear in mind that someone who has significant sway over the outcome of a situation may not be impressed.

8 You need to keep your eyes and ears open for that financial opportunity just around the corner. It's waiting for you.

9 You may be after financial assistance but nobody is willing to give it to you. Are all your figures correct in your proposal or plan?

10 You could be getting conflicting signals from your partner and these need to be clarified. Misunderstandings can easily occur today.

11 A relationship can go stale after a long period of time if it is not kept stimulated and interesting. Is that where you're at?

12 Being together for a long time can make you like a pair of slippers, but that doesn't mean you have to be worn down and tired out.

13 Real estate issues captivate you today. If only to see what's on the market or imagine living somewhere else, this could be the day to visit a property auction for fun.

14 You're probably letting your heart rule your head, and that's not such a good idea. You need to be more grounded in your romance.

15 You will opt to stay home rather than party out on the town. Friends may regard you as a wet blanket, but it's best not to follow the crowd today.

16 An exciting new friendship has opened doors to activities you once deplored. There is a sporting aspect to this transit.

17 Energising and invigorating each other is one of romance's great benefits. Being on the same wavelength is a heady experience.

18 There could be distractions from friends or work colleagues just when you are fighting a deadline. Their support may be needed.

19 Make sure you get the recognition you deserve for the hard work you've put into that project. Receiving the credit is important.

20 Today you may be given advice by well-meaning friends and relatives, but in the end your own instincts will prevail.

21 Frustrating Mars and Saturn dominate your personal relationships sphere. You need to bite your tongue rather than antagonistically react to provocation.

22 A deep and meaningful discussion will lift a friendship to new levels. Don't be afraid to reveal a secret, even if you are a little embarrassed.

23 Learning the art of lovemaking will be on your mind today. All of a sudden your perception of a sexual episode will become crystal clear.

24 Higher learning, a new form of study and other cultural pursuits will be on your mind. Commence a different course of learning.

25 You may be exasperated right now, especially in the area of your life in which you want to make progress. Take care and push ahead.

26 You need to make a budget and stick to it. Yes, it's hard to do, but the rewards will be amazing. Maybe even an overseas holiday!

27 Your restless feelings could simply be the result of a messy house or office space. Remove the clutter from the offending area and clear the air.

28 You may be finding it hard to stick with the systems in place at work, but they're there for a good reason, even if it is not apparent.

29 Friendship and profit overlap today. A new business idea can blossom through the help of a close friend. Sharing is the key word.

30 A social event puts you in touch with many new contacts who can be beneficial to your future financial interests. Networking can pay handsome dividends.

31 Finding yourself in the company of younger people will generate a great deal of self-confidence. A youngster in your family has some information.

⤳ SEPTEMBER ⤳

Monthly Highlight

You will want something new in your life. Uranus will prompt you to step outside your normal zone of comfort, particularly between the 2nd and the 7th. Home affairs are buzzing after the 11th, with exciting news on the work front after the 16th.

1 There may be some awkwardness with that new person in your social circle, but you should spend some time getting to know them better.

2 You may be nervous today. Relax a little and don't be too concerned with what others might think of you. Be yourself and exhibit a little courage in the face of opposition.

3 Friends may offer you heaps of advice in an attempt to influence you to accept their spin on things. Always think for yourself.

4 You may be a little intense with those around you at the moment and be seen to be self-absorbed. Explain where you are coming from.

5 It's quite okay to pamper yourself and give yourself a little extra reward today. The law of the universe says that as soon as you love yourself, others will start loving you as well.

6 You may be experiencing material and financial challenges that are not necessarily going the way you would like. Be patient and open to change.

7 A chance meeting with an old friend revives pleasant and unpleasant memories. Filter out the negative and focus on the positive.

8 You need to get out. Forget about sitting behind a desk today. Air your brain and enjoy a short journey, even if it's just to do some window-shopping. It will do you the world of good.

9 You may have information about a work or social situation that someone else is just waiting for you to divulge. Be careful not to spill the beans and be branded a gossip.

10 Your mind is going round in circles like a record. You may be concerned over a loan or some bills. Focus on work, and things will smooth over within a day or two.

11 You may feel awkward speaking about personal matter to someone in your family. Be tactful and, if necessary, avoid the topic completely. Females could be of nuisance value.

12 If your partner or friend seems cold, give them space. Don't superimpose your feelings on the situation. Some time out will bring them back around with a fresh new perspective on things.

13 You may need to concentrate on some issues in your romantic life that have been left unspoken so far. Be kind and especially tactful when broaching the subject.

14 You're planning changes in your workplace. Run these schedules by your co-workers and boss before implementing them. You don't want to get egg on your face if they are not accepted.

15 You can shine brightly in your place of employment, but shouldn't do this at the expense of someone else. A clash of egos or, at the very least, some fierce competitiveness, may have to be dealt with.

16 A new Moon today heralds the beginning of some exciting new professional opportunities. Don't dismiss suggestions from a friend who has more experience than you. It will help you in the long run to listen.

17 Energising and invigorating each other will inspire you and your partner today. Being on the same wavelength offers financial benefits, especially if your partner has been lacking confidence professionally.

18 Issues of commitment are never easy to deal with, particularly if you are in a relationship with someone who is avoiding this path. You may need to make the serious decision, whether to stay with them, or leave.

19 You have an immense drive to uncover the truth today. But you mustn't use a sledgehammer to bust open a walnut. Speak calmly and patiently about what you want your lover or partner to reveal.

20 Issues of money, shared resources and other factors surrounding savings could be sensitive. Don't sweep these issues under the rug or things could blow out of proportion.

21 A revival of your spiritual instincts can be a good thing today. It's probably best to keep internal revelations a secret, or others could think you have gone mad. Let your actions speak louder than words.

22 It could be one of those days where you spend a lot of time getting nothing done. Try to make sure you have a clearly defined objective and a list of what you must get through. Even if you only achieve something small, it's better than nothing.

23 Any feelings of hurt that you exhibit now to your superiors will indicate a weakness in your character. Be strong and keep a straight face under duress. You'll come out on top.

24 There are places you'd like to go today, but work commitments will not allow you to do so. This could build up pressure and frustration as a result. Take your mind off it; focus on the job at hand, and enjoy the day once you turn off your computer.

25 If your friends insist on going places you can't afford—even though they know that—then maybe you need a change now to have things your way, socially speaking. Speak up.

26 Don't let differences of opinion ruin a night out on the town. Friends will be chatty but may oppose some of your opinions on topics that should be avoided.

27 The ground may be moving beneath your feet and you may not quite know how to deal with life today. Sometimes psychological analysis and intellectual deduction confuse you more. Trust the process of life and go with the flow.

28 You may hear a secret that is not pleasant, especially if it relates to someone you love or, worse still, yourself. Reacting is the last thing you should do. Let it slide and try to find the source of the information. That will probably shock you more.

29 Putting things in order is necessary today. You could have a pile of old books, photographs and ancient memorabilia you haven't looked at for years. Tidying up, as well as enjoying a little nostalgic emotion, means you can kill two birds with one stone.

30 The full Moon in your Sun sign indicates the completion of a cycle. A deeper understanding of yourself can be reflected in the way you deal with others more maturely. Some of these people may not understand you, but remember, that is their problem, not yours.

✕ OCTOBER ✕

Monthly Highlight

For singles, this is a month when a new love affair could commence around the 15th. You have more self-confidence and an emotional connection with others. Journeys on the 5th or 6th give you some light relief, with professional matters taking a turn for the better after the 20th.

1 Tempers can flare and words, once spoken, can never be recalled—remember that. You need to be sure if what you're fighting about is really worth it. Actually, are you even sure what you're fighting about?

2 You may make a verbal faux pas, or something you said will be repeated in the wrong context. Plain speech is needed, but don't be too defensive, as this will make you come across as being in the wrong. Always say less than necessary.

3   It's not a good idea for you to burn the candle at both ends just now. Regroup, prioritise and use your diary for time management as much as you do for social get-togethers.

4   Trying a new venue for entertainment can sometimes bring you in touch with a whole new range of people and experiences. This is the time to explore those possibilities.

5   Harmony in a relationship sometimes takes a supreme balancing act. That is okay, as long as both of you are doing the balancing together—willingly! Don't try to impose your will on anyone else.

6   You've tolerably resolved a problem someone has played with your emotions. Go back through your mental history to analyse why the relationship ended up where it did. You are probably just as guilty as the other party. You are responsible for the complications you find yourself in.

7   Your sunny disposition can be used to help a friend in need today. Lack of clarity, or an unresolved issue that someone brings to you, will be cleared up by your positive approach and genuinely compassionate attitude. Home matters take precedence later in the day.

8 Family matters weigh heavily upon your mind and require extreme patience and self-control. You may have heard the same old story over and over again, but to keep the peace, you may need to listen to it just one more time.

9 You can be generous with your feelings at the moment and possibly say or give away too much, only to later regret it. There is someone waiting for you to notice them, but it's probably better to play a little hard to get.

10 Mars will lift your energy today, and you are also in a lucky mood. This is the perfect time to get out your address book and reconnect with friends, acquaintances and work colleagues who have been on the backburner for a while.

11 Watch your mouth, as your words could not only irritate but actually offend someone you're in touch with today. You take centre stage, and all eyes are upon you—you must be beyond reproach and set the perfect example.

12 There may be financial pressures on you at the moment, so there is no reason to go out and spend dollars you don't have. On the other hand, spending money on a wise investment, especially if it is not going break the bank, is an excellent idea.

13 Your financial health may not be too great at the moment, and if you spend more than you earn, that's where you are bound to get into trouble. A professional financial planner can help you clear up the problem.

14 Having different tastes and styles can make a romance interesting, but when it comes right down to it, what do you have in common? You'll need to assess the common ground to have a continuing relationship.

15 You'll soon be able to create new ideas in either your social circle or your workplace. People will look to you for a new direction, and this will bolster your ego to a new level. You're also likely to create a deeper friendship with someone through your business affairs or career.

16 You may be a little self-absorbed or flat in your mood today, and someone will be trying to cheer you up. Biting their head off is not going to win you any Brownie points, is it? They are only trying to help. Appreciate the good gesture.

17 You probably realise by now that not everyone sees things your way, but it shouldn't be a matter of your way or the highway. Be a little lenient when dealing with others, even if you know you are correct in your assessment.

18 Your decisions based on money today may not be completely clear. Postpone any promises. The Moon at this time doesn't deny you a business partnership—it's just that the timing's not the best. Wait a little bit longer.

19 You are confronted with a dilemma at work today. Your desire for success is at odds with your best ethical and moral interests. It requires you to think of the long-term ramifications of any decision.

20 You can't force the hand of fate or destiny today. You may be impatient regarding professional or financial matters, but hold on to your horses. Good things come to those who wait.

21 Your incredible focus is admirable, but you may be a bundle of energy with nowhere to go. Try pouring that power into some more effective planning until the right opportunities present themselves later. You are still feeling somewhat impatient.

22 Don't take a situation too seriously today. Not everything is meant to be taken seriously. On the other hand, a friend may be oversensitive to some of your remarks. Try to be aware of the best possible response so as not to offend anyone.

23 You are self conscious with friends today because the topic of discussion seems way over your head. It's best to listen and learn rather than trying to assert yourself when you are ill equipped to do so. Your modesty will be respected in lieu of intelligence.

24 Find a solution to a problem. However, it really requires a deeper understanding before you become resolved. You'll probably ask yourself how you got into a financial pickle. You need to go back and clearly identify your motivation for spending. Getting an overview of things will reveal the answer.

25 There are plenty of stimulating opportunities for social and commercial benefits today. You simply have to pick up the phone and be proactive. Laziness may be setting in, so try not to succumb to this negative emotion.

26 You have a great capacity to see the best in most situations, and today is no exception. Look behind the façade and see the truth. Not everything you see should be taken at face value. There are benefits in hidden things.

27 Your mind is a little restless and likely to be erratic in its responses to the demands of loved ones. You must try to see things from their perspectives before jumping down their throats.

28 Invite your peers to a creative and innovative think-tank today. Share new ideas using the group. There is power in numbers just now.

29 Professional circumstances are a welcome relief from the pressures of home life and social activities. These can also be lots of fun when mixing with people and learning more about life, giving you a sense of accomplishment.

30 A surprise introduction to a friend-of-a-friend may well be just the one you thought you would never meet—and, of course, don't forget to thank that friend!

31 Personal strength and integrity are your key words just now, and improving yourself interests you. Self-help books, meetings, lectures or simply discussions with friends will activate an intense desire to develop yourself.

❧ NOVEMBER ❧

Monthly Highlight

Venus makes its presence felt in your zone of personal and marital relationships. This is a great omen for your love life, and means things are much smoother, especially after the 10th. Jupiter's influence affects your relationships in a positive way, and things are back on track.

1 You can try telling another person what to do, but don't be surprised if they disagree! Freedom of choice is a wonderful thing, and you need to respect that in your conversations today and tomorrow.

2 Friction can creep into a relationship if the lines of communication are not kept open. Any doubts you have will need to be voiced politely today.

3 Going through life joined at the hip may not be to everyone's taste, and it is okay to have some time alone—for your own soul's sake—from time to time.

4 House hunting is on the cards just now, and the planets bring out your curiosity and desire to see what possibilities are available in terms of an alternative domicile. Look around, but don't make a premature decision.

5 You can enjoy emotional satisfaction and harmony in your home life. Relationships with women run especially well. If you have a solid emotional base in your life, you will receive the benefits of these family relations.

6 In a new relationship it is often the everyday and the mundane that let you see the other person in a less-than-starry-eyed light.

7 Even though you're a little wild and woolly, you can still enjoy good health and get out and about, meeting new people today. A disappointment in the arena of love doesn't mean you're out of the game permanently.

8 Additional expenses encroach on your capacity to enjoy the moment. You've certainly overspent or been careless in factoring costs into your budget, so you're behind the eight-ball. This is not the end of the world, but you will have to hold off on a few anticipated social adventures to get back on top of things.

9 Financial matters require some crucial meetings, after which you can safely move forward with your plans. However, have a backup plan in place, because there could be an unexpected twist—one that requires you to think quickly on your feet.

10 Doing things mechanically will be a most uncomfortable experience, but certain social obligations require it today. If you find yourself in an uneasy circumstance, a certain amount of pretence may be the only way to get through the situation.

11 Make room in your special relationships for people who have been in your life for a long time. Love should not be exclusive, and you need to pay attention to that just now.

12 There's sexual chemistry with a newcomer today. Things can get rather hot, and this gives you the possibility of developing a fully fledged love relationship. With your sexual planets activating you, anything's possible.

13 Joining hands does not necessarily mean joining bank accounts! Keeping separate accounts is smart until you feel totally committed to the other person.

14 Travel plans are not a bad idea, but it's best to travel with someone to keep you company. Even though you prefer independent exploration, find someone who has similar interests and your journey will be worthwhile.

15 Home is where the heart is. You will have made a domestic change previously but didn't think it through. If you've landed yourself in an environment where you feel like a fish out of water, you need to reconsider your options.

16 The new Moon of the 13th is exceptionally satisfying and continues to bring new professional ideals into focus. Adjustments in your workplace, including the comings and goings of new bosses and employees, create an interesting but somewhat tenuous environment for the time being.

17 Financial changes could result in loss or setbacks that force you to explore new strategies and plans for your future. It's possible that these adverse situations are not under your control, but are caused by general economic conditions. Do everything in your power to minimise any speculative losses. Be more conservative in your monetary affairs.

18 Your psychic abilities get stronger at this time and you can use your intuition, along with your influence, to achieve an edge on your competitors. Practise makes perfect.

19 You need to talk with friends who can give you insights on re-evaluating your current relationship. Their words of advice will be comforting just now, but, more importantly, will help you deal with this ticklish problem.

20 A quiet night out—dinner with friends—can help you reconnect with someone you haven't seen in a while, or make a new acquaintance with someone who seems to have a lot in common with you. Don't refuse the invitation—otherwise you could regret it later when you learn what was on offer.

21 You're feeling passionate; you want to express your love and you have so much to offer romantically. But what's holding you back? Forget about your lover's or friend's reactions at this time.

22 A quieter period is marked today during a quiet phase. This is a chance for you to investigate the more spiritual and solitary parts of your nature. New inspirations can follow, and solutions to problems that have been difficult will mysteriously come to you.

23 You will come across as having great charisma and magnetism today. Friends and colleagues will just want to be near to you. Don't let others suck the life out of you, though.

24 You may have a great desire to break down barriers that have stood between you and someone you are attracted to. However, you may need to take the initiative to get the ball rolling.

25 You may be able to solve your long-standing problem by simply listening to the other person and considering the matter from their side. Empathy is your key word at present.

26 You may have to be first to offer an apology, but it will be accepted and things will return to normal. Little things can mean a lot.

27 The focus is again on money, with your finance ruler in an excellent position today. There are several opportunities staring you in the face, but you've overlooked them. They could pay handsome dividends. Check your past transactions and ferret out these valuable pathways.

28 Memories of the past will be weighing heavily on your mind and this is the result of someone's careless words. Don't take these matters to heart, but by all means learn from your experiences.

29 Someone with whom you have been in touch for a long while will surprise you with a new opportunity. They could propose you a deal that you have secretly only dreamed of. This may come as a complete surprise, but is something you will definitely investigate.

30 You have to use a high degree of courage to break free of limiting circumstances just now. You must speak your mind to a family member to bolster your confidence. Working with your partner will obviously make your workload much easier.

❧ DECEMBER ❧

Monthly Highlight

Focus on making significant changes to your living quarters this month. Venus and Saturn indicate loans, finances and other matters of insurance. Friends are instrumental in helping you understand the intricacies of money between the 11th and the 15th.

1 A friend's erratic behaviour will cause confusion for you this month. You have to look beyond their superficial antics and understand the deeper implications. Rather than addressing their behaviour, rest assured that helping them with another personal problem might be a more appropriate approach.

2 Real estate deals and other investments today will provide you with a source of renewed income. Stabilising your family life and offering your immediate family circle financial security will also be high on your agenda.

3 A chance meeting is lucky. New relationships commence for you. Unusual people—or those who are not your cup of tea—will peculiarly attract you.

4 A lucky break occurs today. You'll be in two minds about whether to accept an offer due to its financial benefits—the social and emotional ramifications of the decision may be another thing altogether. You'll be balancing material rewards with emotional benefits at this time.

5 It isn't the best moment to secure a loan or increase your limit on a credit card. It could be one of those days where the forces of nature conspire against your every move. Wait until you have more information and do some comparative shopping before attempting the financially impossible.

6 Make a sacrifice, put aside a large slab of money and pay off those niggling debts. You can lavish some extra luxury on yourself now, but that will only make the debt and worry worse for you. Curb your appetite.

7 A heavy onset of intense activity in your life may come to a grinding halt when your body tells you to slow down. Do so, because you'll require every ounce of vitality to sort out a financial matter. Have plenty of rest during this phase.

8 On a personal front, there is the desire to deepen the level of honesty in your business relationships. Clear away anything that is impeding the coming together you seek.

9 Your popularity is strong, as is your public approval. You have a few days of this powerful energy on which to capitalise. Spruce up your outfit, create a new hairdo and look your best, because unexpected opportunities will require you to make a lasting impression.

10 Today, confront someone over a money matter. The way in which you raise the issue will be equally important, because a certain amount of hostility over the whole affair is indicated.

11 If you're feeling criticised and upset by the insensitive words of a friend, you must simply gain control of your feelings to get through it. You have a feeling there's an ulterior motive, but you're probably making a mountain out of a molehill. Self-control is not necessarily easy, but its application and success offers you great personal power.

12 Your excitement could cause others to feel as though you're talking *at* them rather than *with* them. Be sensitive to how others perceive you because this is a favourable time for making friends and forming new alliances. An invitation to travel is also quite likely.

13 Educational pursuits are strong for you at this time. You could be confused, or you may need to rethink some of your strategies. Your investigations will cause a little stress or strain. Try to gather information in a more relaxed manner.

14 Matters take a solemn turn when sad news reaches you. The misfortune or difficulty of a friend could require your compassionate assistance. Help friends or relatives: it will divert you, but this will be something you choose to do.

15 Your intellectual and verbal skills are most recognisable. Although you might make a great impression on someone at that meeting or lunch engagement, be cautious if their flattery seems a little over the top. Apart from getting a big head, there may be other reasons for their compliments.

16 It's likely you'll make considerable headway in your social circumstances today. Expect things to progress quickly when your social life moves into a higher gear.

17 Lots of social and cultural events are featured for you. Recreational trips and journeys with friends will give you a sense of satisfaction. For now you should use this stress-free period to get on top of things, especially if you've been on edge.

18 Neptune is causing you to be muddle-headed and not think clearly. Work decisions should be weighed up carefully until you're thinking clearer. Work alone rather than cluttering up your personal space with other people's energies today.

19 Communicating with long-forgotten friends or those who have, in the past left, your locale and moved interstate or overseas is likely. On the other hand, if you need to buy a gift or offer a token of appreciation to someone, purchasing something that has a foreign feel about it will be perfect.

20 You'll be running yourself into the ground today. Take time out to recharge your batteries, because too much of a good thing will end up costing you in terms of your health and vitality.

21 This is a time in which your physical drive is strong. You won't want to be hanging around sitting behind a desk in the last week of the month. It's time to get out and about and have your blood pumping.

22 There are prospects for exciting and challenging times just now. Clear the backlog of work filling your in-tray, though. Letting chores build up will cause you to miss a vital financial opportunity that arises at this time.

23 You have to dig deep to draw out the power of your imagination. Sharing your ideals with others, especially loved ones, will make you feel as if you are at odds with them. You don't need to justify your creativity.

24 Your financial position, or at least your attitude towards it, is subject to some dramatic swings when Mercury opposes your finance zone. Be careful not to allow impulse to rule your decisions where spending is concerned. Check prices by comparing offers before committing yourself.

25 Your relationships with work colleagues are in a quandary. Your ideas and theirs just don't seem to gel. You will also feel slightly embarrassed. A dominant male figure will be the source of this problem.

26 You pick up the pace and are extremely busy again. There's a growing restfulness, and this relates to your relationships, too. Seeking new partners, or something different, will occupy your mind.

27 As much as you'd like to advance your ambitions, you'll find resistance and changes of heart in those who'd previously given you reassurances. Adjustment will be the key to keep things moving along.

28 Home improvements and other domestic issues have slipped through the cracks. Eyesores around the home need fixing. Decorating and refurbishing will catch your fancy, and you'll create a more pleasant living environment for yourself.

29 Work matters may leave you a little high and dry because pressure is the last thing on your mind. Your relationships will be more harmonious, though.

30 A lightning-fast infatuation with someone is likely. Your ruling planet, Mars, is likely to initiate some action in this direction. Love is certainly in the air.

31 Sexual desires begin to get stronger as Venus activates your personal relationships and deeper physical wants.

2012
ASTRONUMEROLOGY

HE WHO DIES WITH THE MOST
TOYS, IS, NONETHELESS, STILL DEAD.

Anonymous

THE POWER BEHIND
⌁ YOUR NAME ⌁

It's hard to believe that your name resonates with a numerical vibration, but it's true! Simply by adding together the numbers of your name, you can see which planet rules you and what effects your name will have on your life and destiny. According to the ancient Chaldean system of numerology, each number is assigned a planetary energy, and each alphabetical letter a number, as in the following list:

AIQJY	=	1	Sun
BKR	=	2	Moon
CGLS	=	3	Jupiter
DMT	=	4	Uranus
EHNX	=	5	Mercury
UVW	=	6	Venus
OZ	=	7	Neptune
FP	=	8	Saturn
—	=	9	Mars

Note: The number 9 is not allotted a letter because it was considered 'unknowable'.

Once the numbers have been added, you can establish which single planet rules your name and personal affairs. At this point the number 9 can be used for interpretation. Do you think it's unusual that many famous actors, writers and musicians modify their names? This is to attract luck and good fortune, which can be made easier by using the energies of a friendlier planet. Try experimenting with the table and see how new names affect you. It's so much fun, and you may even attract greater love, wealth and worldly success!

Look at the following example to work out the power of your name. A person named Andrew Brown would calculate his ruling planet by correlating each letter to a number in the table, like this:

A	N	D	R	E	W		B	R	O	W	N
1	5	4	2	5	6		2	2	7	6	5

And then add the numbers like this:

1 + 5 + 4 + 2 + 5 + 6 + 2 + 2 + 7 + 6 + 5	=	45
Then add	4 + 5 =	9

The ruling number of Andrew Brown's name is 9, which is governed by Mars (see how the 9 can now be used?). Now study the Name-Number Table to reveal the power of your name. The numbers 4 and 5 will play a secondary role in Andrew's character and destiny, so in his case you would also study the effects of Uranus (4) and Mercury (5).

Name Number	Ruling Planet	Name Characteristics
1	Sun	Attractive personality. Magnetic charm. Superman- or superwoman-like vitality and physical energy. Incredibly active and gregarious. Enjoys outdoor activities and sports. Has friends in powerful positions. Good government connections. Intelligent, spectacular, flashy and successful. A loyal number for love and relationships.
2	Moon	Feminine and soft, with an emotional temperament. Fluctuating moods but intuitive, possibly even has clairvoyant abilities. Ingenious nature. Expresses feelings kind-heartedly. Loves family, motherhood and home life. Night owl who probably needs more sleep. Success with the public and/or women generally.

Name Number	Ruling Planet	Name Characteristics
3	Jupiter	A sociable, optimistic number with a fortunate destiny. Attracts opportunities without too much effort. Great sense of timing. Religious or spiritual inclinations. Naturally drawn to investigating the meaning of life. Philosophical insight. Enjoys travel, explores the world and different cultures.
4	Uranus	Volatile character with many peculiar aspects. Likes to experiment and test novel experiences. Forward-thinking, with many extraordinary friends. Gets bored easily so needs plenty of inspiring activities. Pioneering, technological and creative. Wilful and obstinate at times. Unforeseen events in life may be positive or negative.

Name Number	Ruling Planet	Name Characteristics
5	Mercury	Sharp-witted and quick-thinking, with great powers of speech. Extremely active in life: always on the go and living on nervous energy. Has a youthful outlook and never grows old— looks younger than actual age. Has young friends and a humorous disposition. Loves reading and writing. Great communicator.
6	Venus	Delightful and charming personality. Graceful and eye-catching. Cherishes and nourishes friends. Very active social life. Musical or creative interests. Has great money-making opportunities as well as numerous love affairs. A career in the public eye is quite likely. Loves family, but often troubled over divided loyalties with friends.

Name Number	Ruling Planet	Name Characteristics
7	Neptune	Intuitive, spiritual and self-sacrificing nature. Easily duped by those who need help. Loves to dream of life's possibilities. Has healing powers. Dreams are revealing and prophetic. Loves the water and will have many journeys in life. Spiritual aspirations dominate worldly desires.
8	Saturn	Hard-working, ambitious person with slow yet certain achievements. Remarkable concentration and self-sacrifice for a chosen objective. Financially focused, but generous when a person's trust is gained. Proficient in his or her chosen field but a hard taskmaster. Demands perfection and needs to relax and enjoy life more.

Name Number	Ruling Planet	Name Characteristics
9	Mars	Extraordinary physical drive, desires and ambition. Sports and outdoor activities are major keys to health. Confrontational, but likes to work and play really hard. Protects and defends family, friends and territory. Has individual tastes in life, but is also self-absorbed. Needs to listen to others' advice to gain greater success.

YOUR PLANETARY
✕ RULER ✕

Astrology and numerology are intimately connected. Each planet rules over a number between 1 and 9. Both your name and your birth date are governed by planetary energies. As described earlier, here are the planets and their ruling numbers:

1   **Sun**

2   **Moon**

3   **Jupiter**

4   **Uranus**

5   **Mercury**

6   **Venus**

7   **Neptune**

8   **Saturn**

9   **Mars**

To find out which planet will control the coming year for you, simply add the numbers of your birth date and the year in question. An example follows.

If you were born on 14 November, add the numerals 1 and 4 (14, your day of birth) and 1 and 1 (11, your month of birth) to the year in question, in this case 2012 (current year), like this:

Add 1 + 4 + 1 + 1 + 2 + 0 + 1 + 2   **= 12**

1 + 2   **= 3**

Thus, the planet ruling your individual karma for 2012 would be Jupiter, because this planet rules the number 3.

YOUR PLANETARY
⤫ FORECAST ⤫

You can even take your ruling name number, as discussed previously, and add it to the year in question to throw more light on your coming personal affairs, like this:

ANDREWBROWN =   9

Year coming   **=**   2012

Add 9 + 2 + 0 + 1 + 2   **=**   14

Add 1 + 4   **=**   5

Thus, this would be the ruling year number based on your name number. Therefore, you would study the influence of Mercury (5) using the Trends for Your Planetary Number table in 2012. Enjoy!

Trends for Your Planetary Number in 2012

Year Number	Ruling Planet	Results Throughout the Coming Year
1	Sun	**Overview**

Overview

The commencement of a new cycle: a year full of accomplishments, increased reputation and brand new plans and projects.

Many new responsibilities. Success and strong physical vitality. Health should improve and illnesses healed.

If you have ailments, now is the time to improve your physical wellbeing—recovery will be certain.

Love and pleasure

A lucky year for love. Creditable connections with children, family life is in focus. Music, art and creative expression will be fulfilling. New romantic opportunities.

Work

Minimal effort for maximum luck. Extra money and exciting opportunities professionally. Positive new changes result in promotion and pay rises.

Improving your luck

Luck is plentiful throughout the year, but especially in July and August. The 1st, 8th, 15th and 22nd hours of Sundays are lucky.

Lucky numbers are 1, 10, 19 and 28.

Year Number	Ruling Planet	Results Throughout the Coming Year
2	Moon	**Overview**

Overview

Reconnection with your emotions and past. Excellent for relationships with family members. Moodiness may become a problem. Sleeping patterns will be affected.

Love and pleasure

Home, family life and relationships are focused in 2012. Relationships improve through self-effort and greater communication. Residential changes, renovations and interior decoration bring satisfaction. Increased psychic sensitivity.

Work

Emotional in work. Home career, or hobby from a domestic base, will bring greater income opportunities. Females will be more prominent in your work.

Improving your luck

July will fulfil some of your dreams. Mondays will be lucky: the 1st, 8th, 15th and 22nd hours of them are the most fortunate. Pay special attention to the new and full Moons in 2012.

Lucky numbers include 2, 11, 20, 29 and 38.

Year Number	Ruling Planet	Results Throughout the Coming Year
3	Jupiter	**Overview**

Overview

A lucky year for you. Exciting opportunities arise to expand horizons. Good fortune financially. Travels and increased popularity. A happy year. Spiritual, humanitarian and self-sacrificial focus. Self-improvement is likely.

Love and pleasure

Speculative in love. May meet someone new to travel with, or travel with your friends and lovers. Gambling results in some wins and some losses. Current relationships will deepen in their closeness.

Work

Fortunate for new opportunities and success. Employers are more accommodating and open to your creative expression. Extra money. Promotions are quite possible.

Improving your luck

Remain realistic, get more sleep and don't expect too much from your efforts. Planning is necessary for better luck. The 1st, 8th, 15th and 24th hours of Thursdays are spiritually very lucky for you.

Lucky numbers this year are 3, 12, 21 and 30. March and December are lucky months. The year 2012 will bring some unexpected surprises.

Year Number	Ruling Planet	Results Throughout the Coming Year
4	Uranus	**Overview**

Overview

Unexpected events, both pleasant and sometimes unpleasant, are likely. Difficult choices appear. Break free of your past and self-imposed limitations. An independent year in which a new path will be forged. Discipline is necessary. Structure your life appropriately, even if doing so is difficult.

Love and pleasure

Guard against dissatisfaction in relationships. Need freedom and experimentation. May meet someone out of the ordinary. Emotional and sexual explorations. Spirituality and community service enhanced. Many new friendships.

Work

Progress is made in work. Technology and other computer or Internet-related industries are fulfilling. Increased knowledge and work skills. New opportunities arise when they are least expected. Excessive work and tension. Learn to relax. Efficiency in time essential. Work with groups and utilise networks to enhance professional prospects.

Year Number	Ruling Planet	Results Throughout the Coming Year

Improving your luck

Moderation is the key word. Be patient and do not rush things. Slow your pace this year, as being impulsive will only lead to errors and missed opportunities. Exercise greater patience in all matters. Steady investments are lucky.

The 1st, 8th, 15th and 20th hours of any Saturday will be very lucky in 2012.

Your lucky numbers are 4, 13, 22 and 31.

Year Number	Ruling Planet	Results Throughout the Coming Year
5	Mercury	Overview

Overview

Intellectual activities and communication increases. Imagination is powerful. Novel and exciting new concepts will bring success and personal satisfaction.

Goal-setting will be difficult. Acquire the correct information before making decisions. Develop concentration and stay away from distracting or negative people.

Love and pleasure

Give as much as you take in relationships. Changes in routine are necessary to keep your love life upbeat and progressive. Develop open-mindedness.

Avoid being critical of your partner. Keep your opinions to yourself. Artistic pursuits and self-improvement are factors in your relationships.

Work

Become a leader in your field in 2012. Contracts, new job offers and other agreements open up new pathways to success. Develop business skills.

Speed, efficiency and capability are your key words this year. Don't be impulsive in making any career changes. Travel is also on the agenda.

Year Number	Ruling Planet	Results Throughout the Coming Year
		Improving your luck
		Write ideas down, research topics more thoroughly, communicate enthusiasm through meetings—this will afford you much more luck. Stick to one idea.
		The 1st, 8th, 15th and 20th hours of Wednesdays are luckiest, so schedule meetings and other important social engagements at these times.
		Throughout 2012 your lucky numbers are 5, 14, 23 and 32.

Year Number	Ruling Planet	Results Throughout the Coming Year
6	Venus	**Overview**

Overview

A year of love. Expect romantic and sensual interludes, and new love affairs. Number 6 is also related to family life. Working with a loved one or family member is possible, with good results. Save money, cut costs. Share success.

Love and pleasure

The key word for 2012 is romance. Current relationships are deepened. New relationships will be formed and may have some karmic significance, especially if single. Spend time grooming and beautifying yourself: put your best foot forward. Engagement and even marriage is possible. Increased social responsibilities. Moderate excessive tendencies.

Work

Further interest in financial matters and future material security. Reduce costs and become frugal. Extra cash is likely. Additional income or bonuses are possible. Working from home may also be of interest. Social activities and work coincide.

Year Number	Ruling Planet	Results Throughout the Coming Year
		Improving your luck
		Work and success depend on a creative and positive mental attitude. Eliminate bad habits and personal tendencies that are obstructive. Balance spiritual and financial needs.
		The 1st, 8th, 15th and 20th hours on Fridays are extremely lucky this year, and new opportunities can arise when they are least expected.
		The numbers 6, 15, 24 and 33 will generally increase your luck.

Year Number	Ruling Planet	Results Throughout the Coming Year
7	Neptune	

Overview

An intuitive and spiritual year. Your life path becomes clear. Focus on your inner powers to gain a greater understanding and perspective of your true mission in life. Remove emotional baggage. Make peace with past lovers who have hurt or betrayed you. Forgiveness is the key word this year.

Love and pleasure

Spend time loving yourself, not just bending over backwards for others. Sacrifice to those who are worthy. Relationships should be reciprocal. Avoid deception, swindling or other forms of gossip. Affirm what you want in a relationship to your lover. Set high standards.

Work

Unselfish work is the key to success. Learn to say no to demanding employers or co-workers. Remove clutter to make space for bigger and better things. Healing and caring professions may feature strongly. Use your intuition to manoeuvre carefully into new professional directions.

Year Number	Ruling Planet	Results Throughout the Coming Year
		Improving your luck

Maintain cohesive lines of communication and stick to one path for best results. Pay attention to health and don't let stress affect a positive outlook. Sleep well, exercise and develop better eating habits to improve energy circulation.

The 1st, 8th, 15th and 20th hours of Wednesdays are luckiest, so schedule meetings and other important social engagements at these times.

Throughout 2012 your lucky numbers are 7, 16, 25 and 34.

Year Number	Ruling Planet	Results Throughout the Coming Year
8	Saturn	

Overview

This is a practical year requiring effort, hard work and a certain amount of solitude for best results. Pay attention to structure, timelines and your diary. Don't try to help too many people, but rather, focus on yourself. This will be a year of discipline and self-analysis. However, income levels will eventually increase.

Love and pleasure

Balance personal affairs with work. Show affection to loved ones through practicality and responsibility.

Dedicate time to family, not just work. Schedule activities outdoors for increased wellbeing and emotional satisfaction.

Work

Money is on the increase this year, but continued focus is necessary. Hard work equals extra income. A cautious and resourceful year, but be generous where possible. Some new responsibilities will bring success. Balance income potential with creative satisfaction.

Year Number	Ruling Planet	Results Throughout the Coming Year
		Improving your luck

Being overcautious and reluctant to attempt something new will cause delay and frustration if new opportunities are offered. Be kind to yourself and don't overwork or overdo exercise. Send out positive thought-waves to friends and loved ones. The karmic energy will return.

The 1st, 8th, 15th and 20th hours of Saturdays are the best times for you in 2012.

The numbers 1, 8, 17, 26 and 35 are lucky.

Year Number	Ruling Planet	Results Throughout the Coming Year
9	Mars	**Overview**

Overview

The ending of one chapter of your life and the preparation for the beginning of a new cycle. A transition period when things may be in turmoil or a state of uncertainty. Remain calm. Do not be impulsive or irritable. Avoid arguments. Calm communication will help find solutions.

Love and pleasure

Tremendous energy and drive help you achieve goals this year. But don't be too pushy when forcing your ideas down other people's throats, so to speak. Diplomatic discussions, rather than arguments, should be used to achieve outcomes. Discuss changes before making decisions with partners and lovers in your life.

Work

A successful year with the expectation of bigger and better things next year. Driven by work objectives or ambition. Tendency to overdo and overwork. Pace your deadlines. Leadership role likely. Respect and honour from your peers and employers.

Year Number	Ruling Planet	Results Throughout the Coming Year

Improving your luck

Find adequate outlets for your high level of energy through meditation, self-reflection and prayer. Collect your energies and focus them on one point. Release tension to maintain health.

The 1st, 8th, 15th and 20th hours of Tuesdays will be lucky for you throughout 2012.

Your lucky numbers are 9, 18, 27 and 36.

The World of Mills & Boon®

There's a Mills & Boon® series that's perfect for you. We publish ten series and with new titles every month, you never have to wait long for your favourite to come along.

Blaze. — Scorching hot, sexy reads

By Request — Relive the romance with the best of the best

Cherish™ — Romance to melt the heart every time

Desire™ — Passionate and dramatic love stories